MW00622763

TENT
FOR SEVEN

a camping adventure
gone south out west

MARTY OHLHAUT
WITH GRACY LY

SANDRA JONAS
PUBLISHING

Sandra Jonas Publishing House
PO Box 20892
Boulder, CO 80308
sandrajonaspublishing.com

Copyright © 2023 by Marty Ohlhaut with Grace Ly

All rights reserved. No part of this book may be used in any form whatsoever without the written permission of the publisher, except for brief quotations included in critical articles and reviews.

Printed in the United States of America
28 27 26 25 24   2 3 4 5 6 7 8

Book and cover design by Sandra Jonas

Publisher's Cataloging-in-Publication Data

Names: Ohlhaut, Marty, 1950–, author. | Ly, Grace, 1980–, author.
Title: Tent for Seven: A Camping Adventure Gone South Out West / Marty
 Ohlhaut and Grace Ly.
Description: Boulder, CO : Sandra Jonas Publishing, 2023.
Identifiers: LCCN 2023937222 | ISBN 9781954861107 (hardcover) |
 ISBN 9781954861114 (paperback) | ISBN 9781954861138 (ebook)
Subjects: LCSH: Ohlhaut, Marty, 1950– — Travel — Canadian Rockies (B.C.
 and Alta.) | Canadian Rockies (B.C. and Alta.) — Description and travel.
 | LCGFT: Travel writing. | Autobiographies. | BISAC: TRAVEL / Canada
 / Western Provinces (AB, BC). | BIOGRAPHY & AUTOBIOGRAPHY /
 Personal Memoirs.
Classification: LCC F1090 .O35 | DDC 917.1104
LC record available at http://lccn.loc.gov/2023937222

Photography credits: vii, Flavijus Piliponis/Adobe Stock; 65, Mike Moruzi; 79, nathandanks.com/Adobe Stock; 237, Visual Branding Agency. All other photographs are from the authors' private collections.

To Joeline

contents

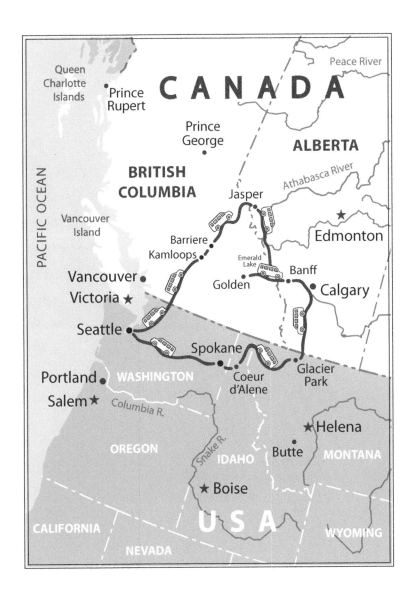

The 1994 Ohlhaut Vacation Route

authors' note

Marty Ohlhaut

Immediately after the events that unfolded in this book, I found myself perched over my keyboard night after night, pecking viciously until the early morning hours. I recorded our camping excursion to the Canadian Rockies as a way to sort through my emotions and to reconcile myself to everything that had happened.

The more I typed, the more I remembered of previous ventures into the great outdoors: the conquests, the consequences, the twists of fate. Not all of my audacious expeditions were self-inflicted—I had several willing accomplices over the years.

As I flipped through the pages, I felt a great sense of relief—the weight of our disastrous vacation was now off my chest.

Grace Ly

Many years ago, I came across the notes my father wrote after our family trip to Canada. Interspersed throughout were stories of adventures he'd had in his youth—unbelievable experiences I never knew about. These tales were almost too outlandish to be true and needed to be told.

I approached my father, and together we worked diligently to bring his stories to life in this book. I fact-checked details and researched locations. We were going to change the names of his friends to spare them embarrassment, but that wasn't necessary—the names he used were authentic nicknames his friends had acquired along the way for things they had done to embarrass themselves.

We did change the names of a few other people mentioned in this book, but that is all we changed. Their descriptions are accurate, their kindness, probably understated.

The names of my family members have not been changed, and their characters are portrayed as they were in 1994 when this story takes place. We had no cell phones then, Google didn't exist, and you had to stop and ask for directions if your paper map couldn't get you there. It was a different time. The majority of the stories from my father's youth took place in 1972—a very different time indeed, a different society, a different world.

Now in his seventies, my father continues to live a life full of adventure and travel. He has, admittedly, made a few questionable choices along the way (who of us hasn't?) and, quite frankly, is lucky to be alive—as are some of his traveling companions.

In *The Proud Highway*, Hunter S. Thompson writes:

Life should not be a journey to the grave with the intention of arriving safely in a pretty and well-preserved body, but rather to skid in broadside in a cloud of smoke, thoroughly used up, totally worn out, and loudly proclaiming, "Wow! What a Ride!"

This is the story of my father's ride.

1.

grin and bear it

Welcome to the wilderness.

When you're lying on the ground with your eyeballs about four inches above the dirt, a baby possum ambling your way looks like a voracious carnivore. Watching a five-hundred-pound bear approach from this angle will paralyze you. I wanted to warn the others, but I was as rigid as an I-beam, unable to speak. Snapping branches had woken me to the sight of a lone bear illuminated by the full moon over the Sierra Nevada. He passed within inches of my face, his stench so rank it almost pried me from my rigor mortis.

I stared at his little stump of a tail as he lumbered away from me and over toward my four sleeping friends. He headed straight for Woody, sprawled out on top of the picnic table, and effortlessly flipped the table sideways. Woody went soaring. He landed with a thud and let out a yell that ended abruptly when he caught sight of the perpetrator.

The bear slobbered and grunted about for a bit and then went for our heavy-duty, fifty-pound cast-iron cooler. With one flick of his paw, that cooler was thirty feet down the dark road. One more swipe and the cooler was in the nearby creek. In no time, the bear had ripped it open and was chowing down on about $350 worth of freshly purchased groceries.

By now everyone was wide awake, and we scrambled into our van and pursued the beast down to the creek. When we got his rump square in our headlights, we began honking and screaming and gesturing like lunatics, trying to scare him off. He looked back at us, then wheeled around and reared up, facing off the van—all eight feet of him, his immense paws and claws spread wide. Our jaws hit the floorboard. He let out a deep roar that darkened our shorts. This bear could have peeled off the top of the van and snacked on us like sardines.

We timidly extinguished our headlights, quietly reversed the van, and backed meekly into our campsite. Still watching the bear, we turned off the ignition, and no one moved. That's where all five of us stayed the rest of the night, trying in vain to sleep, while listening to the sounds of our dinner guest enjoying his buffet.

At dawn, we ventured down to the creek to survey the damage, expecting to see the cooler in pieces. But it was remarkably still intact, just slightly dented on one side. Likewise, the lid, flung about fifteen feet downstream, was still usable, though it brandished a couple of deep scratch marks across the top. Perhaps Yogi had some experience in opening heavy-duty coolers. Bits of plastic and containers were scattered about, but every shred of food was gone.

As we broke camp later that morning, we were annoyed by all the leaves and twigs sticking to our boots and pants. And then we uncovered the reason for our nighttime visitor: Mel admitted to pouring honey all over the ground and beneath the picnic table in a juvenile attempt to attract a bear to our site.

The four of us gaped at him, not sure how to exact recompense for such a boneheaded move. But we all concurred—something had to be done. We considered tying Mel to a tree for a night and pouring honey all over him. Seemed a little extreme. Was voted down three to two.

We were largely in favor of having him replenish the groceries our bear friend just polished off. But considering our dire financial straits, including Mel's, this approach probably wouldn't have yielded much. Instead, adopted by a four-to-one vote, we ragged on Mel continuously over the next several hours, along with the next few days, bandying his name about rather disrespectfully. As this process continued, his name morphed from Mel to Melon Head. This seemed judiciously brutal.

In fairness to Mel, all of us had grown despondent over our lack of animal sightings. We had been on the road for four weeks and hadn't come across a single creature worth writing home about. From the moment we graduated from the University of Cincinnati and hatched our plan to go west for the summer, we had talked about the bears and other wildlife we would see along the way. But the only things we had spotted so far were some deer droppings and what appeared to be raccoon tracks.

Frankly, I was relieved about not seeing bears, though I would never have told the guys. Yes, I wanted to see wolves, moose, coyotes, and elk, but not bears. After a nose-to-nose run-in with a couple of cubs four years earlier, I would have been happy if the entire species had gone extinct.

Even so, the honey debacle opened the floodgates. Woodland animals started appearing everywhere, including more bears—much to my horror and everyone else's delight. And they visited us without any encouragement from Mel.

Our moonlight skirmish with the bear was just one of many unforgettable memories we collected that summer. I loved waking up in the woods, cooking over a campfire, going where the road took us, and falling asleep under the wide-open skies. A simple life, immersed in the intoxicating pleasures of the outdoors: hiking along a fresh mountain stream, watching the sky transform into a kaleidoscope of colors as the sun set, and listening to the wind rustle the tops of the pines. I felt a kinship with nature I'd never known before.

At the end of August, as my buddies and I rolled back into Ohio, thirteen states and thirteen thousand miles under our belt, a radical new plan was taking shape in my mind. Forget working in an office. I would move to California and become a park ranger. It was impossible for me to wrap my head around doing anything else.

Without a doubt, our trip to the Wild West in 1972 had been the best time of my life. Sure, I had a few bruises. And I had run out of money. And I was still deathly afraid of bears. But for a guy from the Midwest, there was nothing like it. And I couldn't wait to go back.

Now, here I was, two decades later, getting ready to take my five children to the Canadian Rockies for a two-week camping trip. Well, five children, fifteen bags, three boxes of hand-chopped firewood, two coolers, one monstrous tent, and one enthusiastic, if somewhat cautious, wife.

And cautious for good reason. I'm not always the most practical guy to live with, especially for a former nursing instructor like Joeline. She has seen firsthand a lot of the mishaps I've narrowly avoided. As I have freewheeled through life, she has proceeded with thoughtful vigilance.

I had just arrived home, enduring another long day at the office. My job at IBM kept me busy close to sixty hours a week, overseeing a large group of project managers, all dealing with hyperactive schedules and hard deadlines. And before a vacation, I had to put in even more time devising plans to keep everything under control while I was gone, including, sadly, a schedule for calling Seth, my point man. (The Europeans do this right. When they go on vacation, they vacate. We simply relocate.)

I had long since abandoned my ambitions of becoming a park ranger. Meager salaries and small, antiquated housing made me re-think my plan. It would have been difficult to raise a family that way. Instead, I landed a decent-paying job at IBM in North Carolina that allowed us to travel to the big, beautiful parks throughout North America. After our youngest was born six years before, Joeline and I had to accept that we wouldn't be whisking off for lavish vacations to the French Riviera on one income. So we came up with an alternative: camping. It was the best means to an end—that end being the ability to explore exciting places for which we barely had the means. The kids loved sleeping in a tent, Joeline loved being outdoors, and I loved not going broke.

The house was quiet, everyone asleep. I poured a shot of scotch over a single ice cube and went into the living room. The floor was awash with the expansive spread of our luggage and camping gear. After all the trips we had taken over the years, Joeline had mastered the art of organization and efficiency. I never had to worry about broken equipment, a forgotten tool, or a misplaced item.

I picked up the receipt from Jesse Brown's Outdoors lying on the table. Two new sleeping bags. In red pen, she had drawn a smiley face next to "You saved $20.00." It always amazed me how committed Joeline was to getting the best possible deal.

She had been packing and stacking for a week with the help of our oldest daughter, Julie, who was fifteen and the most respon-sible one of our kids. She was also the most reluctant camper of the brood, but was always willing to give Joeline a hand with any undertaking.

After nearly two years of planning, I couldn't believe we'd finally be leaving soon. Sixteen long, relaxing days camping in the beautiful Canadian mountains and forests.

But getting there would be anything but relaxing.

I regretted again not calling a year in advance instead of only eight months (who would have thought?) to get a decent nonstop flight from Charlotte to Seattle. Even with all our frequent flyer miles, we couldn't do better than a 6 a.m. departure. Brutal. I looked at my watch. We'd have to get up in less than five hours.

I dreaded to think what a 4 a.m. wake-up call would do to my kids, along with a six-hour flight and a three-hour time change. They'd be jet-lagged zombies by the time we landed.

Still, we had seats together on the same flight, so we lucked out there. That was far better than splitting up the family and taking two different planes, the way we had on our trip to California two years before.

I got down on the floor and checked everything. Shoehorning all our supplies into twenty-one pieces of luggage had been nothing short of a magic show. Back then, USAir allowed three checked bags per passenger, a nicety soon to be abandoned by all airlines. Thank God for large, ever-expandable duffel bags—limited only by the audacity of the packer and brawn of the bearer.

Looming large in the middle of all our stuff were my storied hiking boots. Weighing in at about fifteen pounds each, they were industrial sized and built to withstand the apocalypse. They were bigger than most ski boots. They were bigger than some ski *boats*. My trusted companions for twenty years, they had carried me to the top of Longs Peak, Mount Whitney, and the Middle Teton. (I know—who travels all the way to Wyoming and then only scales the Middle Teton? After my friends and I watched helicopters airlifting stranded hikers off the icy slopes of Grand Teton, we altered our course.)

The boots were completely waterproof, fireproof, bulletproof— and most importantly bear-proof—whatever that means. Although in retrospect, they weren't completely waterproof, nor were they all that comfortable. Especially on a cross-country flight crammed into a tiny coach seat. At my size—six foot four—there's nothing comfortable about any plane ride unless you're sitting in first-class, sipping a cocktail. But wearing the boots was more practical than packing them.

On the coffee table, Joeline had neatly assembled all the personalized AAA maps, laying out every mile of our proposed journey. Invaluable. That is to say, they're pure gold when you're on course and amazingly worthless when you aren't. If I'm tempted to veer off onto the back roads we come across, Joeline will rein me in. "Can't we just stay on course, Martin." Whenever she addresses me as Martin, anything else in that sentence is not to be taken as optional.

I moved on to the three heavy boxes of firewood and made sure they were extra secure. But I didn't have to worry—Joeline always used massive amounts of duct tape and added a makeshift handle to the top.

The night before, when we tallied up everything, it turned out we could get two more checked items onto the plane. Since we still had plenty of logs lying around our yard thanks to Hurricane Hugo, I went out into the drizzle and fog and split up five more, even though we already had one large box bursting around the edges.

"Marty, what are you doing?" Joeline said, as I walked back into the house. "We don't need any more firewood—or any of the ants and termites and beetles that go with it."

I shrugged. She was probably right, but the kids loved piling logs onto the campfire at night, and I couldn't bear their disappointment when we ran out of combustible fuel right at the height of a roaring inferno. Plus, she had called me Marty, so I probably had some leeway.

After downing the last of the scotch, I climbed the stairs to get a few hours of sleep. Given how absent I'd been from my family of late, with the ungodly hours and pressures, I was eager to start my hard-earned sabbatical. Getting back to nature, to the great outdoors, was exactly what I needed.

Camping had always brought us closer together, whether on our trips to the local mountains or to the distant Pacific Coast. I was looking forward to that.

All in all, it was shaping up to be our ultimate camping vacation, our biggest and potentially last blowout expedition as a whole family.

I wanted it to be extra memorable. The little guys, Max and Angela, wouldn't be little much longer, and the older girls, Julie, Grace, and Mollie, born within three years of one another, were already talking more about boys than about bears. Mom and Dad were more to be tolerated than appreciated.

Had I known just how memorable our trip was about to be, we never would have left the house.

2.

into the woods

Enjoying watermelon slices on the roadside in the Great Smoky Mountains.
Left to right: Mollie, Grace, Max, me, Julie, and Angela.

On Thursday, July 28, 1994, we arrived at the Seattle-Tacoma International Airport, and miraculously so did all twenty-one pieces of luggage, in pretty much the same condition as when we left Charlotte. I can't say the same about us.

None of us had slept except Angela, our youngest, who was now bright-eyed and bushy-tailed. Joeline, Julie, Mollie, and I drooped and shuffled, while Grace and Max were wired with fatigue. Thank God for Angela. She was our beautiful, benign blessing and the only one with snow-white locks, giving her an angelic appearance to match her personality.

Next mission: take possession of the van at Rent-A-Wreck.

I turned to Joeline. "This should only take a few minutes." I feigned a stoic smile and took off to find the shuttle, feeling a little criminal for leaving her alone with our mountain of luggage, four girls, and one wild boy. Max was a happy eight-year-old, with explosive energy and excitement, and when fueled by a lack of sleep and inestimable anticipation, raging insanity was just around the corner.

The fellow behind the rental counter looked like he'd been in a fight—and lost. Maybe several fights. His left eye, at least I presumed there had been an eye there at one time, was swollen shut and ringed with purple and black bruises.

He advised me matter-of-factly that our fifteen-passenger van was ready to go, except for one minor detail. A rate adjustment of a thousand dollars. Upward.

Why were adjustments always upward? Was the state of his eye the result of another customer's recent upward adjustment?

"Hold on." I unfolded the paperwork and showed it to him. "I have the details right here in writing."

"That's nice." The guy didn't even pretend to read the contract. "But we're gonna just have to wait for Hank to straighten this out."

"Who's Hank?"

"The office manager."

"Sorry, but I can't wait for Hank. I've left a horde of untamed children rampaging through the airport. I gotta get back, pronto."

By the blank look on his face, he was clearly unmoved. But since he had already inattentively tossed me the keys, I turned to go. "Tell Hank I'll call him."

Just as I reached the door, it swung open wildly and in stepped a huge hulk of a man with "HANK" embroidered above his chest pocket.

Oh, Christ. There went the thousand dollars.

But thankfully, Hank was a cerebral man. Seeing the terms printed out clearly in the contract, he said, "We're good to go. You know, you're getting a great deal on this van. For another great deal, head on up to Larry's grocery store and tell 'em Hank sent you. And make sure to use Rent-A-Wreck again in the future."

"I will." And indeed we did.

Our van was easily distinguished in the Rent-a-Wreck lot. It was, in fact, the only van in the lot—an ugly gray behemoth that sagged to the left. I had to laugh. If the driver's door didn't come off in my hands, I was taking off with it—no questions.

The door remained on its hinges, and I rushed back to the airport, half expecting by now to see security guards chasing my kids up and down the tarmac. Instead, as I pulled up to the curb, I was greeted by the usual antics. Angela was climbing atop our pile of bags, spreading the lower ones across the sidewalk. Max had latched onto a suitcase like a monkey while Grace pulled it, running as fast as her skinny little legs could carry her, both laughing hysterically. Julie and Mollie were lying spread-eagle on the luggage, acting like they'd just crossed the Atlantic in steerage. Joeline was standing watch close by not looking nearly as frazzled as the scene warranted.

While I corralled the kids and ushered them into the van, Joeline stuffed all our gear into the inadequate storage space, filling every nook and cranny, somehow manufacturing space where none had been.

We had planned to load up with as much food and supplies as possible to avoid paying wilderness outpost prices after crossing the Canadian border. With a bit of trepidation, we took Hank's advice and drove up the road to Larry's. There was a picture of Larry plastered right next to the store entrance—he bore an amazing resemblance to Hank.

We grabbed three shopping carts and dispersed down the aisles. Joeline and Angela were in charge of the hearty sustenance, like hot dogs, sausage, hamburger patties, and lunch meat; the three older girls, cereal and chips; and Max and I, everything else. Hanging on to the front of the cart, my overzealous son kept telling me to go faster as I loaded up with paper towels, tissues, and toilet paper and then picked up a couple of cans of lighter fluid, matches, and the last bottle of lamp oil for our four lanterns.

We converged with the rest of the gang at the checkout. Joeline and Angela had amassed enough meat to make a carnivore gag and several bags of ice to keep it fresh. The girls' cart was chock-full of Cheez-Its, Gold Fish, and Cheetos, along with bags of marshmallows, bars of chocolate, and boxes of graham crackers for s'mores, not to mention several boxes of cookies and sugary cereal. Joeline didn't allow junk food at home but was lenient on vacations, and the kids took full advantage of that.

Larry and a couple of his brothers spent several minutes stuffing the thousand dollars' worth of procurements on top of and in between the kids, who were nestled across the back seats, simultaneously giggling and groaning about this arrangement. I covertly stashed all the flammables inside the back door to reduce the likelihood of untimely combustion.

Finally! We were ready to get the show on the road. I steered the van north out of town and up into the mountain wilderness, each of the kids clutching their favorite bag of munchies. As we gained altitude, the scenery grew more beautiful and panoramic.

The tension was just leaving my body when a sudden loud pop came from the back seat. "What the hell was that?" My eyes shot up to the rearview mirror.

"My Cheetos exploded!" Max screeched in delight.

I looked over my shoulder and saw Cheetos everywhere and ravenous kids going after them. "You're telling me that the bag just randomly popped open? That you had nothing to do with it?"

"Dad," Julie said, "all the bags are getting bigger."

"What?" Just then, I opened my mouth wide to pop my ears, and it dawned on me what had happened. More eruptions were only a few additional feet of elevation away.

"Let them explode!" Max said, shoving several Cheetos into his mouth. "Then we won't have to open them ourselves." He smiled a giant smile, exposing his two large front teeth, now coated in a dusting of orange.

As the other kids shouted their agreement, Joeline turned in the passenger seat, doing her best to stifle a grin. "Absolutely not," she said.

"I can fix this," Mollie said with more confidence than any twelve-year-old has the right to possess. She tossed her long, thick hair over her shoulder, removed her earring, and used it to poke tiny holes in all the remaining chip bags—delaying their consumption by at least a couple of days.

"Gee, thanks a lot, Mollie," the other kids groaned in unison.

As the sun was setting, we drove across the Canadian border, three hours from Kamloops, our final destination for the evening. Getting there had taken almost twice as long as I had originally calculated, which I should have anticipated due to my mediocre scheduling and estimating skills.

I had been driving for a while and needed a break, so I pulled over, and we all got out of the van to admire the view. I couldn't help but notice how vast and serene the surroundings had become, just as we had hoped.

All was good—except for my feet. They were killing me. Encased in boots for twenty-four hours, they needed a respite. After much grunting and straining, I managed to pry my feet out of the mammoth clodhoppers, and I placed them down in the door well, closed the door, and drove bootless into the evening.

My stomach was growling as we pulled into Kamloops. Instead of looking for healthy dinner options, I pulled right into the Whippy Dip, knowing this would be a big treat for the kids—for me too. And it would probably take us right to the brink of what Joeline referred to as our "garbage food intake."

The kids all talked at once about what they were going to get, each trying to outdo the other in extravagance. I was also salivating over the possibilities. As soon as I parked, Joeline and the kids piled out of the van and rushed over to the window. Before joining them, I reached down into the door well to retrieve my trusty hiking boots.

What the . . . ? Where was my left boot? Panic struck my haggard brain.

I rummaged through all our stuff—but I knew it wasn't there. It was like searching for a boulder in a sandbox—if the boot had been there, I'd have seen it. I must have accidentally knocked it out of the van right before I shut the door. That meant it was some 150 miles back, lying lonely and likely flattened on the side of the road. I leaned against the van and debated going back and scouring the highway. But it was almost ten, and my boot was over two hours away.

My kids stared at me blankly, licking their cones. Joeline patted me on the shoulder. "C'mon, Martin, get over it. We aren't going back. Besides, those boots were disgusting."

So that was it. A retrieval mission wasn't going to happen. To make matters worse, all I had left to wear for the next two weeks was one pair of flimsy tennis shoes. And one right boot, if such a strange need arose.

Bereavement set in. I couldn't function properly for several minutes. I loved those boots—the first and only ones I had ever purchased—even though they never fit quite right. The store didn't have my size when I bought them. For twenty years, I had worn size 13 boots on my size 14 feet. I went through a lot of moleskin because of those faithful boots.

To ease the pain, I ordered a triple cone with extra chocolate and a cherry on top and wandered over to the payphone. I needed to distract myself by focusing on the next task of the evening: securing accommodations for the night. I began calling around to the local lodging establishments only to discover, most incredibly, that every single hotel room in Kamloops was occupied.

How could Kamloops be full? Who had even heard of Kamloops?

Feeling a pang of desperation, I called a hotel up the road in Barriere, praying there would be a vacant room in a town whose dot on the map was smaller than the width of the line for the highway.

"Barriere Dive Inn, Liam speaking." His voice was so lifeless I was sure I had woken him from a deep sleep.

"Do you have any vacancies?"

"There's one room left. But I can't hold it for you. And just so you know, it doesn't have air conditioning."

"Please hold the room!" I said. "We're heading there right now!"

Who cared about air-conditioning? We were in British Columbia. Given that there was only one room left, I'd be forced to play the invisible children trick. Upon check-in, I would bring one or two children into the lobby while concealing the existence of my other three to avoid having to pay a penalty for having seven people in one room. Cramming seven people into one room is penalty enough.

Hard to believe, but the room was still available an hour later when we arrived. It was also hard to believe that any room this far north on the planet could be so hot. I discovered why when I tried to open the windows to get some fresh air—they were nailed shut.

I hastened back to the front office to ask about prying them open. "There's nothing I can do about it," Liam said, shifting the toothpick in his mouth.

I appealed first to his sense of pity, then to his sense of perspiration, by making a big show of wiping my brow.

"Sorry."

He didn't sound all that sorry.

Resigned, I let out a deep breath and glanced around. That's when I noticed the stack of old, reused Pepsi bottles in the corner, all of them partially filled with a brown liquid that was certainly not Pepsi. Misinterpreting the confused look on my face, Liam gestured to the stack. "Take whatever you need."

"Need for what?" The liquid looked like the pond water Julie had used for a biology project.

"Oh, I forgot to tell you." He removed the toothpick and wagged it at me. "You can't drink the tap water in the rooms. So we've provided complimentary drinking water."

Good Lord. "Oh, uh, thanks, but my family doesn't really drink water."

This was a bald-faced lie. My family guzzles water like a storm drain in a summer downpour. But not wanting to seem rude, and not sure how we were going to satisfy one of nature's most essential needs, I grabbed two bottles of the mystery liquid and headed out the door. I didn't envision us actually drinking this curious cocktail, so I didn't mind having to use the bottles to fend off the two Doberman pinschers that chased me across the parking lot.

When I told Joeline the news, she said, "It can't be that bad. Go back and get some."

"Trust me, the water is gross. It's so brown you can't see through the bottle."

Joeline shook her head, mumbling, "First you lose your boot. Then we have to sleep in a sauna. Now we have no water. I hope this isn't some kind of sign."

The three older girls had an entirely different perspective, seeing this as a fantastic opportunity to indulge themselves in the sodas we had purchased for later in the trip—something else normally absent at home.

I was too punchy with fatigue to care. Joeline too. It was pushing midnight and we bedded down quickly, if a bit parched and sweaty. At least we had accommodations, of sorts.

As I lay sweltering in the heat, my mind swirled. We'd had a few mishaps that day, but nothing of any magnitude. Even so, in all of our previous family trips, we hadn't had a single setback.

Although Joeline was the worrier of the group, it did make me nervous to think what would happen if catastrophe struck out here in the wilderness with five kids. Things could turn quickly, as I knew so well from the Wild West trip. But trouble among a group of five guys all in their twenties is more often an adventure, a story to tell around the campfire.

Back in '72, my buddies and I had barely made it out of Ohio when we suffered our first stroke of bad luck. As we arrived in Columbia, Missouri, 450 miles west of Cincinnati, our van began smoking and choking and belching. We had purchased the used vehicle specifically for the trip, our list of requirements not very high—namely, tires, an engine, and an operable steering wheel. Then we made modifications to reflect our exquisite taste: casement windows along the sides, two-by-fours on the roof to serve as luggage racks, old bucket seats bolted to the floor so the van would qualify for passenger license plates, and speakers everywhere there was a gap. One of the guys had even built a commissary into the rear corner.

We were men of meager means, and our investment in this van, however humble it might have been, represented a significant portion of each of our individual fortunes. I had brought along the remainder of my life's savings to fund the trip, about $350.

When the town mechanic told us the repairs would cost around $500, we began choking and belching. I took my turn staggering over in shock to the cashier's window, painfully prying five twenties out of my skinny wallet and handing them over. Since it never occurred to any of us fiscal reprobates to do any substantive financial planning for this trip, we didn't realize the imminent likelihood that we'd all end up waiting tables in some greasy spoon deep in the Utah boon-docks to pay for our return home.

In a poorly disguised effort to get us off the premises, the shop attendant directed us to a small community college right across the street. He assured us the campus was swarming with hot chicks.

We paid a quick visit to the nearby convenience store and then found a nice, peaceful spot on a grassy slope overlooking the lake in front of the college, waiting to be accosted by all those hot chicks. But the campus was deserted. Of course—it was summer. His seductive promise had hijacked our brains. We grudgingly acknowledged we'd been duped. Seeking alternate consolation, we pulled the tabs on our beers and kicked back.

We started out feeling bad about our luck, but as we drank our way through our recent purchase, we became less focused on our misfortune. As the evening wore on, some of us became a lot less focused. Woody, for one, decided it was time to cool off in the lake.

It was early evening and not all that hot. But Woody's internal thermostat was malfunctioning. He bolted upright off the ground, tossed his empty beverage container to the side, and charged down the hill in full dress and dove headfirst into the lake.

Except this body of water wasn't a lake in the traditional sense. It was no more than about six to twelve inches deep at any spot—more of an expanded puddle with a rocky bottom. Woody's feet didn't even get wet. His legs waved errantly in the air—a good sign—at least he could still move them. The ambulance arrived and hauled him to the emergency room, where he received a score's worth of stitches in his face and head. Happily, the doctor said Woody had to stay only one night and then he could continue the trip with us, albeit with a minor headache that would linger for the next ten weeks.

As the sun set on day one of the Wild West trip, our van was in the shop, our finances were in tatters, and we were camped out in a hospital.

I reached over to the nightstand where one of the girls had left an open soda can and took a big swig. It was warm and flat—the opposite of refreshing. I sighed and rolled back over in bed. Despite my lost boot and the hellish motel room, our first day in Canada hadn't been all that bad.

Our vehicle was operational, we weren't broke, and no one was in the hospital. Yet.

3.

love at first sight—in the nude

Mel flashing the Rockies.

A bead of sweat rolled into my eye and woke me at three in the morning. It was a miracle that I'd been able to fall asleep in that inferno. I finally got up and took a cold shower.

Tiptoeing back to bed, I had to do a bit of a sideways jump-step over the kids sleeping on the floor and almost landed headfirst on Julie. She didn't stir, probably sleeping the best of all of us, even under those sizzling circumstances. Julie would absolutely prefer a toasty motel room to a balmy campsite any day.

As I lay down next to Joeline, I could see her face in the orange glow from the streetlight. Even while sleeping a trace of apprehension shone on her face. Her idea of a fun camping trip with the kids involved activities that didn't pose the slightest risk. I always pictured us cheerfully setting up camp together, tromping through the forest enjoying the wildlife, and roasting gooey marshmallows over a cozy campfire. Not Joeline. She pictured the kids hammering tent stakes through body parts, being munched on by a grizzly, and careening headfirst into a burning ring of fire.

She was a real stickler about safety, but she focused her concerns less on herself and more on everyone else: her immediate family, and then her extended family, and then her friends and associates, and then on humanity in general. That's what made her such a wonderful nurse.

The kids were well aware of this. When they wanted to go bungee jumping or skydiving, they asked me for permission, knowing I'd probably like to join them.

As risk averse and cautious as Joeline is, every once in a while, she surprises me—like she did seventeen years before, when she agreed to marry me after dating for a mere three months. Her family warned her not to do it. My family warned her not to do it. It will never last, they said. Slow down, give it more time. Three months isn't nearly long enough to get to know someone.

But I had no doubts she was the one. I knew it the minute I spotted her lifeguarding at the local pool. Tall, slender, blond, sporting the customary one-piece red swimsuit, a life preserver tucked snuggly under her arm. I was hooked.

How could I get her attention? I was about to hurl myself into the pool and flail for help when it dawned on me that there was no smooth way to transition from drowning victim to eligible bachelor. That and I was standing at the shallow end where the water was only two feet deep.

Yes, three months did seem pretty short. But it wasn't nearly as short as the courtship of a guy we met up with on the Wild West trip. He had us beat by a mile. And it all started on a beach in California.

Couzy, one of the more conscientious fellows among the five of us, had a prodigal brother, Pinky, who lived in LA. Not surprisingly, Couzy and Pinky hadn't talked for several years, but we needed a place to crash for a few days. So Couzy, giving into our appeals, contacted Pinky and made plans to meet him at his place of "employment"—the Horseshoe Club in Gardena—a gambling hall complete with armed guards everywhere.

None of us had ever been in a place like that before. We loitered around a bit, halfway looking for Pinky and halfway looking at the piles of chips on the tables, the sullen looks on their owners' faces, the overriding glitzy gloom, and the harem of half-naked barmaids scurrying around with trays full of liquor.

When Couzy finally happened upon his brother, Pinky informed us he had much more "work" to do and that he'd meet us back at his condo later. He gave us a key, told us to make ourselves at home, and not to wait up.

We spent three eventful days exploring Los Angeles, enduring constant ridicule from Pinky, who didn't think we were cool. But when it came time to depart, he hopped into our van and announced that he was going up north with us.

Along the way, he went on and on about the kick-ass beaches at Big Sur, off the Pacific Coast Highway. When he divulged that they were nude beaches, they would, of course, be our first destination. At twenty-two years old and from Ohio, we had never been to a beach, much less a nude one. On our second day up the coast, Pinky led us on a detour that ended at some large sand dunes.

"Okay, boys," he said. "Go burn your eyeballs out." It took us all of about ten seconds to scramble over one another and out of the van and then thirty more seconds to make our way through the low-lying brush and onto the sand.

As the beachgoers came into view, we saw nothing but a whole bunch of people in full bathing suits.

"Hey, what the hell?" Mel asked. We all turned to Pinky and grumbled our complaints.

"Patience, fellas. Keep moving on down the beach."

We walked at a healthy clip around some craggy cliffs, across a slew of slippery, moss-encrusted rocks, until finally, at long last, we arrived. The "free love" movement was very much alive and thriving on that beach.

"Voilá, gentlemen," Pinky said, sweeping his arm wide, his chin held high, just as Moses must have done on Mount Nebo over the promised land.

Voilá? We now understood how the Israelites must have felt looking out over the Dead Sea and its surrounding desolation. Instead of Playboy bunnies prancing around, the beach was littered with regular old, everyday naked people.

We walked down a ways, hoping that the sights would improve. All the while we were trying to appear nonchalant behind our dark sunglasses, cranking our eyeballs around without any telltale turn of the head. The Mexican sombreros we'd bought at Disneyland a few days earlier made us look all the more foolish.

Especially Mel, who had stripped down as soon as we stepped onto the nude beach. I couldn't figure it out, but the guy loved taking his clothes off. It had become a ritual whenever we summited a mountain top or discovered a secluded waterfall or trekked to a scenic lake. We'd all traverse the last few steps to our destination to find Mel, standing stark naked, his arms outstretched, admiring the view. He never missed an opportunity to get into his birthday suit.

That day, I learned one of life's sad lessons: ninety percent of the world's population looks far better in full dress. Every once in a while, a captivating member of the other ten percent came into view, but in general, we were looking *away* a lot more than we were looking *at*.

As a statistics major in college, I was intrigued by the probabilities of the view improving the farther down the beach we went. The law of averages played out in our favor when we came upon a couple of young ladies dashing out into the waves. It appeared they might be in danger in the rough waters, so we donned the appropriate attire—those of us who hadn't already followed Mel's lead—and hurried out to offer our help. Next thing we knew, we were sitting on the beach together, discussing some of the great philosophers in history. All of us traveling cowboys thought this was just a frivolous sortie, but not Pinky. One of the young ladies, Jazmin, had caught his fancy, and in short order, he made his move. Sucking in his ample stomach, he snuggled up close to her, giving her big puppy-dog eyes and whispering in her ear. This went on for about an hour. Then he planted one knee firmly in the sand and asked for her hand in marriage.

Jazmin nodded enthusiastically. "Yes!"

Pinky turned to Mel. "Would you do us the favor of officiating at our wedding ceremony?"

Mel had taken to following Pinky around, laughing at all his jokes and imitating his gestures. "I'd be honored," Mel said, his face beaming, though he was completely unqualified for the job.

Jazmin and her friends knew the perfect place for the wedding—a beautiful pool at the base of a majestic waterfall in the mountains, just across the road from where we were parked. Abandoning the beach, we hustled up a narrow, wooded path to another bathing area au naturel, this one definitely with a stricter entrance policy and a much better viewing ratio—and it didn't take a math major to figure that out.

The people relaxing there were happy to share the spot with the arriving wedding party and joined our joyful celebration. Everyone gathered around Mel and the blushing young couple at the foot of the crystalline waterfall for the sacrilegious ceremony.

Mel uttered a string of unintelligible words apparently intended to unite these wandering souls together for eternity, following up with, "And now it's time for us to honor the union of Pinky and whatever her name is by removing all our clothes and immersing ourselves in the frothing pool of Neptune." Leave it to Mel to direct everyone to get naked. Most of us had already made that adjustment, and we were quickly submerged in the frigid waters of connubial celebration.

Jazmin asked Woody, the only one with a camera, to be the official wedding photographer. The nuptial guests posed freely, giving him some priceless shots—although several of them did attain a monetary value a decade later when certain members of our group demanded the negatives.

After a few final closing comments from Minister Mel and a flurry of fond wishes from the audience, the young couple pranced off down the newlywed trail and faded into the sunset. The brides-maids stayed around for the wedding reception, which was held, open bar, at a nearby campground. We danced and partied until sunrise.

Couzy didn't hear from Pinky again for a couple of years. He wasn't exactly surprised to find out that the passionate lovers had run into irreconcilable differences only a few days into their wedded bliss and had to take divergent paths into their respective futures. That turn of events cast a dampening shadow over my belief in love at first sight.

Compared to an hour-long courtship, my three months with Joeline was a lifetime. And happily, our wedding had a much better outcome.

4.

bear necessities

Mount Robson, BC, Canada. *Left to right*: Julie, Angela,
Grace, Max, Mollie. And Goat.

At first light on Friday, we packed and fled our sweltering room. We needed to hit the road anyway. It was about a five-hour drive to Jasper National Park, and with the weekend starting, I was worried about the crowds, especially given how scarce rooms seemed to be.

Outside the quaint little town of Barriere, we turned north toward the high mountains. The western side of the Canadian Rockies has a more subdued beauty than the eastern slopes and therefore is generally less dramatic. But this was a perfect way to build crescendo to the magnificence that was to come.

After a couple of hours of driving, some residents in the back seats began voicing what would become a common complaint. Max's voice was the most distressed of the group. "I have to *go*. Now!"

This was followed by a chorus of agreement. We were in a part of the world that offered no roadside relief. I hated to stop for anything in our quest to get to Jasper expeditiously, but certain functions can't be put off indefinitely.

The road before us was long, straight, and narrow, bordered by tall pines on either side and seemingly deserted. I pulled over onto a narrow shoulder, and one by one, the kids filed out of the van like soldiers and scurried over to the grassy area to answer nature's call.

While I stood gazing into the thick woods, delighted to be in the cool, fresh air, my eyes relayed to my fatigued brain that an enormous black bear had emerged from the trees across the road and was ambling our way. I watched rather in a stupor as he picked up speed and approached to within about fifty yards of my family, many of whom were squatting with their shorts down around their ankles.

I shifted to near panic in a second, my heart pounding through my chest. What the hell should I do? What the hell *could* I do? At least six hundred pounds of man-crushing flesh would soon be upon us. Bears react unpredictably when confronted with behavior they interpret as aggressive. Actually, they can react unpredictably to any kind of behavior. And I couldn't risk scaring the kids into a frenzy—although Angela might want to give the bear a big hug and Max would probably want to wrestle around with him.

Having no idea what the older girls would do if they saw this approaching Goliath, and not wanting to find out, I calmly, if a bit shakily, called out, "First one into the van—without making a sound—gets a bag of Oreos."

"Me! Me! Me! Watch out!" Max yelled.

"Silently. Please."

"Oh, yeah." He covered his mouth and made a beeline for the side door, his sisters following right behind, with a little pushing and shoving. Cookies were at stake.

The tactic worked. The whole crew maneuvered hastily back into the van as the bear padded into the woods without giving us the slightest hint of acknowledgment. I pointed toward the side window. "Look at that bear over there."

Everyone spun around, trying to catch sight of him. They all began to realize what had just happened—or more importantly, what hadn't happened. And much to her disappointment, Julie didn't even get a glimpse. Everyone else did, though, and the kids chattered wildly in the back seats, Max happily devouring his winning bag of Oreos.

As we drove off, Joeline turned to me, her eyes blinking. "Oh my God. That was way too close."

Mountain peaks began cropping up on the right side, but they appeared mysteriously distant and indistinct. I assumed it was because they were so high and so far away. It lent an eerie, mysterious aura to the entire backdrop.

We finally made the eastward turn that led us to the most northerly spot for our vacation: the town of Jasper. Recalling the AAA brochures that described the wonders of British Columbia, I thought Mount Robson, the highest point in the Canadian Rockies, should have been a whole lot more discernible than it was right then. We stopped at the visitors viewing area to get a glimpse of this magnificent, glacier-covered rock.

Angela tugged on Joeline's arm. "Mommy, why can't I see the mountain?"

I approached a park ranger nearby and asked him.

He looked north at the peak. "It's hardly ever like this, sir. Massive forest fires in British Columbia have dumped huge amounts of smoke into the air." He turned to glance back at me and smiled. "It'll get better in a week or so."

Well, that figured. We spent two years planning this trip—and a few thousand dollars—and we wouldn't be here when the smoke cleared.

Mount Robson may be the most majestic and imposing peak I have ever seen—or not seen. Unfortunately, the pictures we took would also come out looking the same way. That is, you can't see anything, except enough to tell that what you can't see is probably really beautiful, if you could see it, which you can't.

We blazed through Jasper and made our way directly to Whistlers Campground, one of the largest campgrounds in the national park, only to be greeted by a sign we would see over and over again: "FULL/ COMPLET." At first, I thought someone had meant to write "Completely Full," but was struggling with dyslexia, and then I realized it was bilingual. I don't usually understand half of what's written on a sign when it's all in English, so having half the signs in French made getting around town about as easy as deciphering Einstein's crib notes.

So here it was twelve-thirty, early for us, and all 604 campsites were occupied. That's way more sites than the number of rooms in an average hotel. This vacation wasn't going to be very relaxing if we had to arrive at each new campground by eight o'clock in the morning to secure a site. We had chosen British Columbia in general and Alberta in particular because of their remoteness and inaccessibility—because they wouldn't be crowded.

The ranger informed us that if we hurried down the road twenty minutes to Wabasso Campground, which contained 228 sites, we could potentially get there in time to secure a spot. Twenty minutes later, seven sets of eyes glared at another bright orange FULL/ COMPLET sign.

For some reason, mostly despair, I drove into the campground to check it out anyway. When we arrived at the ranger's entry booth, Dolores, sporting her crisp khaki uniform, gave me a perfunctory greeting.

I wished her a good afternoon and asked if, by chance, they had any available sites.

"Yes, sir, there are two yet unclaimed."

I was so delighted and relieved I could hardly contain myself. I didn't even ask why the FULL/COMPLET sign was posted. "We'll take whichever one you think is the nicest, ma'am." I flashed her a big smile.

Dolores narrowed her eyes. "All the sites are equally nice. But if they don't meet your expectations, you're welcome to pitch your tent elsewhere."

I watched her closely, waiting for the slightest indication that she had been kidding. Nothing.

Not wanting to lose the sites, I hurried to break the silence. "Yes, ma'am! We would be most grateful to stay at either one. Thank you so much."

Dolores shuffled through some file cards in front of her and then looked up. "I'm assigning you to C23." She grabbed a pen. "Now, what's the name?"

"Ohlhaut. That's O H L—"

"Hold on," she snapped. "Ole what?"

"Ole-howt." I'd been through this drill a couple of thousand times before, but was enjoying it more that day than usual.

"Okay. So what's the spelling again?"

"O H L . . ." I paused a moment to let her catch up. "H A U T."

"All right. O H L A U T?"

"No, you missed the H."

"No, I didn't. It's right there." She held out the card and pointed with her pen.

"That's the first H. You missed the second one."

"There should only be one H. Spell it again."

The cadence always messed people up, so I altered it a little. "O H . . . L H."

Her mouth fell open as she squinted at the card.

"Tell you what," I said. "Just leave out the second H, and we'll change our name."

"You're not allowed to do that!"

"Sorry, I was just kidding."

This went on for a while, until Dolores finally thought to ask me for my driver's license.

We successfully registered and took off. Tooling along happily to our site, we happened to pass by the other unoccupied site, C1.

"Look how beautiful that is," I said to Joeline. "This is going to be great, isn't it?"

Then a most disturbing thought fractured my high spirits. Certainly Dolores wouldn't have . . . No, she wouldn't, would she?

We hurried on to C23. It looked nothing like C1. Small and uninviting, out in the open, yet with no appreciable views, and small rocks littered the ground. Sleeping on small rocks, or large rocks, is never comfortable. Not that it would have mattered. We couldn't have pitched our seven-person tent anywhere on that tiny site.

Seemed like Dolores was getting the last laugh. I huffed and fumed, the van idling, before a light bulb went on in my head. "Hey, Joel, drop me off at C1. I'll hold it while you go back and switch our registration."

"Nice try!" she said. "I'll stay at C1. You go back to Dolores."

So we compromised. We unpacked some of our gear at C1, and Joeline took the van and kids back to C23 and let them run around while I hid in the bushes near the check-in booth until the rangers changed shifts. Then I registered us at the much more preferable site with a much more pleasant public servant. Who was laughing now?

As Joeline and the kids unloaded the rest of the van, I set about pitching our enormous blue six-sided tent—a complicated, often time-consuming process, but it was worth it. Big Blue made all the difference on our trips.

I'd had no idea they even made something that large. When I had gone to Jesse Brown's Outdoors, I figured I would have to buy two tents to handle all of us, along with some contraption that would connect the two, like adjoining hotel rooms.

But the tall, cheerful eighteen-year-old sales guy said they had a supersized model that would work for us. "I think we actually have one in stock in the back. We don't have it out on display, since, well, it would take up the whole store."

He chuckled while I cringed. How much would this monstrosity cost?

"This is it." He pointed to a blue-lined Eureka! tent in a catalog. "Says it sleeps six adults, so you'll have plenty of room for your whole family plus some gear. It's made of high-quality material. *And* it has this cool awning off the front so you can leave your dirty, smelly shoes outside the tent and they'll stay dry if it rains."

How did he know about my boots?

"I think this is your best option," he said.

"Are there any other options?"

"Not for seven people."

"So this is basically it?"

He nodded. "Uh-huh. But it's a good option, like I said. Having a reliable tent really is essential for camping. It's basically your home away from home. I guarantee you'll love it. Oh, and this one is really easy to set up."

Yeah, right, pal. No portable structure designed to house six people, or rather seven, was going to be easy to set up. Shoot, I had a hard enough time just making the bed.

Even so, I caved, ever the patsy for such an enthusiastic sales pitch. With the money required to buy our home away from home, we could have taken that luxury vacation to the French Riviera, with a stop in Paris on the way. Instead, my purchase would be financing this kid's college tuition.

Marching straight home, I gathered the kids into the front yard and proudly pitched that big blue six-sided canopied tent. One by one, the neighborhood kids ventured outside to watch. Within a couple of hours, three other tents sprang up in nearby yards. Ours, notably, would leave the biggest patch of dead grass. The parents of those kids were upset with us for spawning the tent city. And the neighbors without kids were just as upset about the unseemly additions to the formerly tidy landscape.

We hadn't pitched Big Blue for a while now, and I was taking stock of the gazillion pieces and parts scattered throughout the campsite. There were straight poles and bent poles, long ones, short ones, and multi-piece poles, some corded together, all of them in the wrong place. We had stakes of different sizes, and who knew how many were missing. The ropes were knotted up, twisted, and in total disarray. And what was that crumpled-up extra piece of cloth? Oh, right, it was the all-important rainproof covering. And I totally forgot about the awning until Mollie asked, "Hey, what's this long, funny-looking flap doing here?"

That flap helped us find the front of the tent. The other sides looked very similar—screening from top to bottom that could be totally exposed by unzipping the canvas walls down to the ground. When all the sides were completely unzipped, Big Blue was more like an open-air gazebo.

I couldn't remember where any of the pieces went, but I worked diligently to disguise my ineptitude from the kids. After all else failed, I secretly consulted the moldy two-hundred-page instruction manual stuck to the floor of the tent and then began barking orders to the older girls. When they helped, construction took about thirty minutes. If the little guys wanted to get involved, it took closer to forty-five minutes, which didn't take into account whatever repair time was required due to their help.

As the tent miraculously took shape, I told the kids that I was only consulting the instructions to make sure they were correct.

Our sojourn north hadn't taken us out of reach of the hottest, driest summer ever in western Canada. I was drenched in sweat, mosquitoes buzzing around, and we still had to dig a drainage ditch around the uphill side of the tent to keep rainwater from flowing in or under it. I asked the girls to each grab a shovel and start scratching out a culvert around the front. I had no desire to wake up at three in the morning to a stream cascading through the tent as a storm rolled through.

The tent now pitched, we threw in sleeping bags, air mattresses, duffel bags, suitcases, floor mats, and pillows. As a general rule, the coolers stayed in the van. That way, we'd always have food available wherever we went. But more importantly, if we never took the coolers out of the van, we didn't have to remember to put them back in, reducing the likelihood of luring a bear into our site with the scent of salami, ham, or honey—especially honey.

What was next? The firewood. I made a big show of slicing open one of the boxes with my industrial strength Swiss Army knife to the cheers of the kids.

Max clapped his hands. "Can we start a fire now?"

"Not yet, buddy. Let's wait until tonight." I placed a few of the logs around the firepit to give us something to sit on later. As nice as camping chairs would have been, they were simply too bulky to schlep around. The exquisitely chopped wood would do just fine.

Joeline grabbed the clothesline and stretched it between two trees behind the tent. "Hey, kids," she called out, "let's check out the nature trail we passed on the way in. Stretch our legs a bit."

"You guys go," I said. "I want to get these lanterns ready while it's light. I'll catch up with you in a minute."

I filled the lanterns with oil and stuck one in each of our usual places—on the picnic table, beside the firepit, and on a lamp pole near the van. Then I looked toward the back of our campsite to find a good spot for the last one.

Something big was moving in the bushes.

Oh sweet Jesus—black bear number two!

At least I'm pretty sure it was a black bear. Black bears aren't always black, nor are brown bears always brown. Truth is, you really can't tell which kind of bear you're dealing with by its color. The best way to find out is to climb the nearest tree. If the bear climbs up behind you and eats you, he's probably a black bear. If he stays on the ground and tears the tree down and then eats you, he's likely a brown bear. If he growls horrifically while eating you, he's a grizzly.

The most vicious is the white bear, more commonly known as the polar bear, a sister species to the brown bear, not to be confused with the cinnamon bear, a subspecies of the black bear. And then there is the rarest of them all: the blue bear.

Curiously, the only bear truly discernible by color is the black-and-white giant panda. Strangely enough, it has no interest in eating you. But that doesn't do you any good in North America since pandas live in China.

This particular bear milled about and then started to wander in my direction. Although still several yards away, he was close enough for me to get a substantial whiff. The word "whiff" doesn't truly convey the impact of his aroma—it was more akin to a sordid mixture of skunk spray, freshly decayed rodent, and two-week-old fish.

Incapacitated by a lethal combination of fear and nausea, I just stared at the beast as he approached within swiping distance. But then suddenly, he altered course. Sauntering back off into the woods, he became my favorite kind of bear: the retreating bear.

5.

flying the coop

Riverside lunch in British Columbia.
Left to right: Angela, Julie, Grace, Mollie, me, and Max.

I jumped into the van and fled the scene in search of my family, anxious to find them before the bear did. They hadn't even made it to the nature trail yet. All the kids were crouched down by the side of the road watching several fat-cheeked chipmunks scamper about. Grace was scattering trail mix on the ground.

"I'm pretty sure you're not supposed to feed the critters," I called out the window. "Everyone hop in the van. Let's go somewhere." I kept my mouth shut about the big black critter loitering about.

"What about the Athabasca Falls?" Joeline asked. "I saw a sign a few miles back."

Sounded good. Off we went.

Despite a modest plunge of seventy-five feet, the falls were as violent as any I had ever seen. "Treacherous" might be the best word to describe this spectacle. If an elephant were to somehow plummet into these falls, it's unlikely any trace of the poor creature would ever turn up downstream.

Typically, it takes millions of years for a river to cut down through rocks to form canyons and gorges. In the case of the Athabasca Falls, as furious and compact as they are, it seemed a couple of weeks would have sufficed. To our horror, the cliffs around the waterfall weren't fenced off. Max hollered "Wow, this is so cool!" and bolted forward, stopping only when he reached the edge.

"Max, stay right there!" Joeline yelled. Then turning to me, she said, "You need to put the strap on him."

She was right, of course, but I hated the damn thing—almost as much as he did. As necessary as it was for reminding Max to stay away from the cliffs, it probably would have been of little use had he actually gone over. Reaching into my backpack, I pulled out the wrist band and prepared myself for what was coming. Sure enough, when Max saw me with it, he went into hysterics, his arms flailing, more likely than before to send him over the edge.

"Max, sorry, I gotta hook you up, buddy."

"No, Dad, no, no, no. Please, no!"

I folded like an accordion. It didn't take much. "Fine. You promise to hold my hand and not let go?" This would be more difficult for him than wearing the strap.

But that afternoon, he held on tight and walked around calmly, probably a bit intimidated by the furious falls. It was the rare win-win—and rather heartening.

Back at the campsite, I was surprised—and thrilled—to learn that the Canadian parks provided their clientele with an unlimited supply of *free* firewood. All you had to do was walk to the supply bin and take it. No need to stand out in the rain in the middle of the night hacking away at insect-ridden logs, packing the wood into flimsy boxes, and lugging the decaying cargo three thousand miles.

After a dinner of campfire-cooked sausages, followed by roasted marshmallows, two of the older girls started strolling away from the campsite. Joeline called out to them, "Hey Mollie, where are you two going?" They both burst out laughing. "We don't know where Mollie is. We're just going to get some water." Tricked again. It was actually Grace and Julie. The kids loved it when we messed up their names. And it happened a lot. Partly because they looked like triplets—and partly because we just couldn't remember their names.

It didn't take a genius to figure out that Grace had convinced Julie to help her look for boys. Sure enough, just minutes later, the girls found a tall, freckled, unsuspecting quarry. They strategically placed themselves in his path and played the damsels-in-distress card, insisting there was no way they could manage to carry their heavy water buckets back to their site without his assistance.

Freckles enthusiastically obliged, somewhat reminiscent of the poor helpless creatures our cats would chase and capture and then drag home to show off.

Having caught their prey, the girls quickly lost interest and left him for Joeline and me to entertain. We feigned a trite discussion with poor Freckles, but feeling no connection with the fellow ourselves, we suggested he return to his site to make sure his campfire was being properly stoked.

Now that Freckles might be escaping their clutches, the little damsels reappeared, interested again, and insisted on walking Freckles back to his site.

"Be back in ten minutes, please!" I said.

"Sure," they said casually.

I knew what "sure" meant. Something like "I am acknowledging that I heard words come out of your mouth. I have no idea what they were, nor do I care. I'll simply endure the consequences after I do whatever it is that I originally set out to do, completely disregarding whatever it is that you just said."

Forty-five minutes later, Joeline was frantic. I was enjoying the tranquility so much I hadn't even noticed that the girls were still gone. "We shouldn't have let them walk back with him," she said. "Get in the van and go find them—now!"

"How about you come with me?" Leaving her alone with her imagination could be disastrous. "Mollie, stay here and watch the little guys, would you?"

We climbed into the van and scoured the campground. I started to get nervous myself after we covered the grounds about three times with no sign of the girls or Freckles.

As we passed our site for a fourth go-around, we saw Grace and Julie sitting on the logs by the campfire, innocently roasting their marshmallows as if they'd been there for hours.

In a voice mixed with antagonism and relief, Joeline said to them, "Where the heck have you been? Your father and I have been searching this entire campground looking for you two."

"What do you mean? We've been right here."

Normally a vanishing act like that would have had consequences, but I think Joeline actually enjoyed the girls bringing home their first victim, or catch, I should say. She just didn't want them, or me, to know it. Relieved that all was well, we joined them, emblazing our free firewood and lounging around the campsite. As we listened to the mountain glacier stream roaring in the distance and the cool breezes rustling the tall pines, I watched my older girls talking and laughing and thought back to the summer after I graduated from high school.

My dad was crazy about birds, and he had hung a bluebird house right off our back patio. He spent a couple of weeks clearing out alien nests until two lovely bluebirds, rapt in connubial bliss, set up a homestead there. They hauled twigs, branches, and other nesting paraphernalia from around the neighborhood and disappeared through that itty-bitty hole on the front of their house.

One morning, Dad came rushing in, exclaiming that there were three eggs in the nest. For the next week or so, we anxiously waited for them to hatch. And sure enough, one morning, Dad announced the arrival of three tiny chicks.

Over the next several days, Mama and Poppa would fly in with worms and slugs hanging from their beaks. The moment they left the nest, the little ones would stick their heads out, their mouths wide open, waiting for their folks to return with more grub.

Surely, their flying lessons would commence soon. Learning something as complex as flying would have to take several days of intense instruction, practice, and training. About a week after their birth, I was watching one of the tiny heads poking out of the hole, right after the folks had departed on what I presumed was just another food mission. I was concerned the fledgling would tumble out and crash, Newtonian-style.

Likely just to prove me wrong, he shot out of the house and soared to the telephone wire some sixty feet away, affecting a perfect two-point landing. Seconds later, his brother and sister rocketed from the house in the same projectile fashion. Tarrying only a moment, they soared from the wire and disappeared into the oak trees across the street.

We never saw any of them again.

I had expected to watch them grow up and learn and execute their flying exercises and bond the way families do. But instead, in a single flash, they were all gone—forever.

My little girls were never going to be little girls again. All the wonderful things Joeline had taught me—helping them put on cute frilly dresses, French braiding their hair, telling bedtime stories—all history now. They had flown over to the wire. Soon they would fly into the oak trees.

Angela and Max were still in the birdhouse. Mollie was sticking her head out.

Awash in all this sentimental wisdom, I discovered something else that night. I always thought that if you left oil lamps burning really low in your campsite, they would slowly burn the wick down to the level of the oil, and then the flame would go out. But what really happens is, the wick keeps burning until all the oil in your lamp is gone.

And if that is all the oil you have with you, then you're left in the dark.

6.

silly putty

Elk making themselves at home on the playground,
Jasper, Alberta, Canada.

I don't know how I managed during the Wild West trip, but as time
passed, I found it harder and harder to sleep on the ground. After
two or three minutes in any position, it felt as if the earth were slowly
working its way through my body. An air mattress that comfortably
supported my large carcass made all the difference. It consumed a
sizable chunk of space, but I typically placed it in the middle of the
tent and everyone laid out their sleeping bags around me, making
me the eye of the storm.

That was perfect, unless the thing didn't stay inflated. And I had
no one to blame but myself.

On one of our first camping trips, I had injected a couple of extra
doses of air into the mattress hoping to provide myself with a tad

more support. All was good until I rolled my bulky framework over and carelessly thrust my bony elbow down into the mattress. And I do mean *into* the mattress. As the air streamed out of the hole, tears streamed from my eyes and my derrière sank closer to firm, hard, pitiless Mother Earth.

My mind raced frantically for something, anything to stop the rush of restful repose from my mattress, but as usual, I came up with nothing. The hole was about two inches long and semicircular, roughly matching the contour of my elbow. Our packing tape and Band-Aids certainly wouldn't hold for any length of time. And we couldn't glue anything over a gaping hole like this. We had nothing else that would even stick to the mattress.

Using a flashlight, Julie rummaged around in the younger kids' stuff and pulled out a container of Silly Putty. "Let's just smear this all over the hole."

"That's ridiculous."

"Do you have a better idea?"

She had me on that one. Forever calculating odds and percentages in my head, I was convinced the odds of success fell below the acceptable standard deviation. Nevertheless, we smeared the Silly Putty all across the gash in the mattress and then covered it meticulously with some packing tape and pressed it all down securely in place. To our astonishment, the leaking seemed to stop or at least to diminish significantly.

We spent another half hour reinflating the mattress. Bless Julie's heart. How many teenagers would help out their old man, and do it pleasantly, especially when he had wrecked his own sleeping gear at midnight in the wilderness of Colorado?

Before the mattress flattened itself, I had to get to sleep—and pronto. (There generally seems to be an inverse relationship between the necessity to get to sleep fast and the amount of time it will take to actually fall asleep.) Amazingly, or perhaps only by the mercy of God, I dozed off quickly, and our contrivance held up pretty well throughout the night. By morning, substantial portions of my body had come into direct contact with the ground, but not so much as to discontinue my slumber. I finally rousted out and said, "Julie, you are the greatest."

"Thanks, Dad. I had to do something so we could all get to sleep last night."

Her motivation aside, I figured that if the mattress made it through one night, maybe it would make it through a second, and a third, and so forth. We might have to do a little reinflating, and maybe more taping, each evening, but that certainly wouldn't be enough of a chore to motivate me to properly fix the hole.

So now, two years later, here we were with the same splotch of yellow Silly Putty covering the hole on my hundred-dollar mattress. I felt pretty *silly* when we found the mattress repair kit hiding deep in our storage bin at home just before leaving on this trip. We didn't even know what it was at first, nor that such a thing even existed, but we didn't dare mess with the putty that had served me so well.

After a breakfast of Frosted Flakes and Pop Tarts, we set our sights on Jasper. Normally we tried to avoid the heavily touristed areas, focusing instead on the out-of-the-way destinations. But that day we made an exception.

Originally established in 1813 as a trading post, Jasper is a quiet, quaint resort town that caters to pesky tourists, and judging from the traffic jams and crammed parking lots and packed sidewalks, there were more of them that Saturday than the town had seen in recent history. It took us half an hour just to find a parking space and another half hour to parallel park our sizable fifteen-passenger van.

At the visitor center, one of the rangers helped us sketch out the directions for Medicine and Maligne Lakes, just east of town. She informed us that *maligne* was, ironically, French for "malignant" or "wicked," but that the lake was one of the most stunning and photographed locations in the world.

After pulling up alongside it, I could see why. The scene was quite possibly the most beautiful setting on God's green earth. Tall snow-covered mountain peaks with three distinct glaciers rose in the distance. Out in the middle of the turquoise lake, we saw the small Spirit Island, home to a few Douglas firs. The water was perfectly still, lying in reverence under the deep blue sky. This would be the perfect spot for us to enjoy a picnic.

Julie and Grace carted our meager provisions down from the parking lot while Mollie and Max cleared off a picnic table under some trees to provide shade. Angela was in charge of supervising the entire operation. As we began gobbling down our scant lunch, a substantial congregation of large black birds gathered on the branches overhead. They looked like they were about to swoop down on us, so I said to the kids, "Don't throw any food on the ground or anyplace else where the birds might snatch it. Do you all hear me?"

"Sure, Dad, sure."

Sweet little Grace, always clamoring for excitement and sensing an imminent opportunity for adventure, proceeded to wave her sandwich in the air, apparently to test out my concerns. Before her arm was even fully extended, her PB and J was shredded by several bomb-diving predators. Alfred Hitchcock couldn't have staged it any better.

Her eyes widened as she looked at the remains of her lunch. She sat there speechless. Not so much at what the birds had done, but by the fact that something her parents had warned her about actually happened. Her mouth hung open—and empty.

We finished our lakeside lunch quickly, anxious to leave the fowl kamikazes behind. In our rushed departure, we left lots of crumbs behind for the critters. By the time we reached the van, they had picked the place clean.

A sign posted by the parking lot highlighted a trail that runs along the crest of Maligne Canyon. It turned out to be an unforgettably gorgeous location, especially if you have pictures to remind you of its beauty—which we don't. You must have a camera on hand to take pictures, and I had brilliantly left our camera in the security of the van.

The river had cut a canyon into the earth's crust so steep and narrow that Joeline had to keep Max from hurling himself into the abyss. Threatening to use the safety strap was an ample deterrent. The river, maybe thirty feet across, winds down through the forest through a series of waterfalls, each more impressive than the previous one. As we tramped down the path away from the denser foliage, I was overwhelmed with the beauty of the place and distraught over my photographic malfeasance. I really should have gone back to the van and retrieved the camera. (These were the days when a camera was a separate bulky device—not the omnipresent cell phone of today, which is used to do practically anything except make phone calls.) Unfortunately, as is so often the case, my laziness prevailed.

It was getting late in the day, but there was still time for one last activity. I let the kids vote on their preference, subject, of course, to parental veto. The first nomination was getting ice cream. It passed with a four-to-one vote. Max wanted to find another bear. Off we sped to Jasper, where I bought a half gallon of strawberry ice cream.

Joeline spotted a quaint little park, and I passed out six plastic spoons. The kids ran around enjoying their frozen treat. We were all surprised to see so many life-sized statues of elk scattered arbitrarily around the park. We were even more surprised when the statues started moving around and grazing leisurely. It seems that elk are to Jasper what pigeons are to historical statues—once alluring, but now more of a fertilizing nuisance. The kids loved following them around, and we loved yelling at the kids not to follow them around.

After polishing off the ice cream, we drove to Whistlers Campground. Although they had no available sites, they did have a campfire program, something Joeline particularly enjoyed. This activity won five to zero. Out of curiosity and since we were a little early for the presentation, we took a quick spin through the campground to see what we were missing.

Contradicting the many people who had recommended Whistlers Campground to us, it resembled Plano, Texas, the epitome of flat, postage-stamp lots. The packed campground provided little to no privacy between sites and amazingly no views of the magnificent

Rockies. We counted ourselves lucky to have been routed on to Wabasso, despite the interactions with the lovely Dolores.

The topic for the evening campfire program was coincidentally elk, whose population in Jasper had recently exploded into the thousands. Legally protected there, the elk flock to the town to avoid the more dangerous mountains where bears, wolves, and mountain lions like to eat them. I would certainly have done the same thing.

The ranger opened the program with a scare tactic. "Elk can be aggressive and attack without warning. The females will violently protect their calves, and the males use their jagged antlers as weapons. Those antlers can spike to four feet long and weigh up to forty pounds. Never get close to an elk—and never follow one around."

The ranger scanned the audience. "Okay, I need a volunteer. Who would—"

Max was on the stage before he could finish the sentence. The ranger gave him about a hundred feet of rope and asked him to stretch it out into the parking lot. I thought at first he was just trying to get rid of Max—not necessarily a bad idea. Actually, the ranger wanted to demonstrate how far away a person should remain from the elk—about twice as far as our kids had been.

On our way back to the van, Max jumped around, grabbing my arms and Joeline's, swinging back and forth, overjoyed at having been onstage, or more precisely, offstage, way offstage, but still the presumed center of attention. The girls laughed, patting him on the back, telling him how funny he was, being careful not to make it sound like an actual compliment. Those were difficult to come by in this group.

As the family snuggled together in diverse stages of drifting off to sleep in Big Blue, I could hear the Athabasca River churning in the distance and prayed that my air mattress would hold up for yet another night.

7.

summit fever

Cavell Ice Cave beneath Angel Glacier.
Left to right: Grace, Julie, and Max.

We all put on our Sunday best—that is, anything that was reasonably clean and not too rank. When you're on vacation, there's always the temptation to vacate from everything, including any obligations related to the Sabbath. But we always put forth an effort, some times more diligently than others, to locate a church close to our campground. Now, if the good Lord chose to conceal the whereabouts of the local establishments of worship, we assumed he was granting us permission to forgo the mandatory sacrament.

Not this time. We had spotted a church in Jasper the previous evening, noted the mass schedule, and thus were able to continue our long-standing tradition of arriving late and disturbing the entire congregation while we searched for a place to sit.

We finally took seats in three different locations. Due to poor execution on my part, I ended up alone in the first pew. Typically, I distracted Max in church by playing thumb wars, but that day, I was riding solo right up front in the house of God.

The priest gave a short, simple sermon—too short for me to get a decent amount of shuteye. I usually try to listen to the first part of the sermon, which in turn contributes to the likelihood of my dozing off during the second part. That's why I like to avoid the front of the church, where it is far more challenging to slumber inconspicuously. Right then, I had no choice but to sit up and stare straight ahead.

The elderly priest had a full head of silvery hair and deep wrinkles that exuded an aura of wisdom. He stood tall behind the lectern, his hands gripping the sides. I couldn't tell if this was for devotional effect or simply to keep him from toppling over.

As he was wrapping up his homily, he adjusted his glasses, cleared his throat, and looked directly at me. I felt the heat of his stare burning on my forehead. Opening my eyes wide, I lifted my head, as if to say, "Go ahead, good Father, I've been listening to every word you've said."

Without releasing his gaze, he imparted his closing words with gravity: "You will be tested by unexpected circumstances and hardships. Deal with them humbly, knowing they're a part of God's plan, and this will help you appreciate all the blessings in your life."

And then it was over. I'd been tricked. I accidentally listened to the entire homily and didn't get a lick of sleep. I couldn't shake the eerie feeling that the priest meant those words for me, as if he'd cracked open a fortune cookie and read my future.

After church, I succumbed to the clamor from the back seats and stopped at a doughnut shop on the edge of town and bought several boxes of assorted goodness to take back to the campground. My mother-in-law had once scolded me about being cheap and not buying enough doughnuts for everyone to have their fill. This was difficult to do with my brigade—they could ingest more pastry than a small battalion of storm troopers. As expected, they scarfed down almost everything, leaving behind just one half-filled box.

I cleared off the picnic table and spread out our map. We were as far north as we had ever been on the North American continent, or on the planet for that matter, and from here we would only be going south. I spotted a prominent peak called Mount Edith Cavell. Bizarre. How many other peaks contain both a first and last name? Mount Peter Rainier, Zebulon Pikes Peak, Mount George Everest? So why Mount Edith Cavell?

Joeline scoured one of our brochures and discovered that Mount Edith Cavell was named—as you've no doubt guessed—for Edith Cavell, a woman who never even set foot in Jasper National Park. In tribute to Joeline's nursing background, she pointed out that Edith Louisa Cavell was a British nurse who ministered to the wounded from both sides during the First World War and helped Allied soldiers escape from German-occupied Belgium. For her good deeds, she was shot to death by a German firing squad. No mention was made about the double moniker, but we just assumed it was to emphasize the femininity of this valiant heroine.

Joeline also read that Mount Edith Cavell is considered by many to be the most majestic mountain in the Canadian Rockies. So we piled into our lopsided van and took off to see for ourselves.

It turned out we weren't the only ones with that plan. The parking lot and the road into it were choked with cars. I dropped the family off at the entrance to the parking lot and retreated almost half a mile before finding a spot large enough for our van, then hotfooted it back to the group.

As usual, my little kinfolk were already engaged in various activities. Max and Mollie were playing king of the mountain on a boulder just large enough to ensure the loser would need medical attention. Julie and Grace were sashaying down the path, obviously boy scouting again. And Joeline, holding Angela's hand, assisted her in balancing across a large wooden railing, keeping one eye on her feet, with the other eye on Max, and a third eye on the older girls.

After Joeline rounded everyone up, we convened a quick powwow and agreed to hike the Cavell Meadows Trail. This wasn't a unanimous decision, of course. Julie and Angela dissented, and Joeline registered a vote of "present." But the four-to-two majority ruled and off we went up the trail. I took the lead, carrying the dissenting Angela on my shoulders, and the remaining constituents followed behind, Joeline keeping rear guard. An itinerant bystander could easily have mistaken us for the von Trapp family crossing the Alps. Unless we were to break out in song. We did, in fact, occasionally call out in song, but this was specifically to ward off bears—of any color—in the vicinity. Bears typically steer clear of raucous noises.

As we reached the trail's end, even Julie and Angela acknowledged the beauty of the sweeping views. Directly across from us, Angel Glacier clung to the north side of the mountain, lying peaceful and devout, her wings spread wide across the valley. The snow-speckled Rocky Mountains extended out forever, fading gradually from deep purple to hazy violet. The jagged peaks scratched the blanket of thick gray clouds rushing above them. It made for spectacular photography.

I grabbed my camera, which I had remembered this time, and got the family perfectly posed. Then I clicked the button. Nothing happened. I shook and tapped the camera, but still no click.

Seemed that batteries needed to be changed every five years or so. This must have been year six. And these babies were some type of lithium, graphite, carbonized intergalactic specials—not something you could pick up at your local 7-Eleven.

Then I remembered that we had equipped our crew with cheap, disposable Kodaks. "Do any of you guys have your cameras with you?" Grainy pictures would be better than no pictures. But all I got in response were shaking heads.

I was in charge of the camera and camcorder for crying out loud. How did I not plan for this? This question simply got added to the long list of other similar questions. Sick to my stomach, I stood there trying to burn the scene into memory.

Mollie came over and touched my arm. "Dad, I can run back to the van and get my camera if you want."

"Don't worry about it."

"But I can do it. I'll be back in five minutes."

"It'll take longer than that."

"No it won't. Time me."

I handed her the keys and she dashed off. "We'll wait for you down there by the water," I called after her.

The kids had already run ahead to Cavell Pond, eager to begin one of our favorite pastimes—skipping stones—an activity driven by two primary objectives: to skip a stone across the water as far as possible while simultaneously getting your siblings as wet as possible.

As everyone collected stones, Mollie sprinted up to us and handed me her camera and my keys. "Did I make it?" She leaned forward, hands on her knees, catching her breath.

I had unwittingly failed to check my watch when she left. "Yes! You certainly did. With about thirty seconds to spare. Thanks, Moll."

And then the stone skipping commenced. After considerable slinging and splashing from the group, the athletic Mollie proved herself the victor in the first category with four consecutive skips across the still water. Max got an honorable mention in the water displacement category, even though most of the displacement ended up on him. The girls demanded his disqualification for resorting to large rocks instead of flat stones. No matter to him, as long as his sisters got drenched.

Just below Angel Glacier is a large snow field that extends into Cavell Pond. Joeline and I came of age in Ohio, but our kids hail from the sunny south, Texas and North Carolina. Glaciers, icefields, blizzards, and white-outs were all things of lore. As the kids ran around making snowballs and hurling them at one another, Grace hollered out, "Hey, there's an ice cave over here! Come check it out!"

Before Joeline could get to the chasm, all the kids except Julie had ventured several yards into the cavernous deep freezer. I followed closely behind. The temperature plummeted, and a chilling stillness permeated the vast space. I was stunned by the stark contrast from outside.

We had made it about halfway to the back wall when Joeline's voice echoed around us. "Martin! You guys shouldn't be in there!"

Hmm? After I gave this about one and a half seconds' worth of thought, a pang of realization shot through my body. Good God, she was right.

Just then Max came rollicking over to me, his pants and shirt sleeves soaked. "Dad, look. There's a waterfall."

Off to the side, a healthy stream was indeed flowing down along the ice wall, running across the floor, and disappearing into a sink hole. All that water and Max's drenched condition reinforced Joeline's urgent warning. You don't have to tell me twice (well, I suppose sometimes you do). Casually entering an ice cave, beneath a massive, vertical hanging glacier, under thousands of tons of rock and ice, on a relatively warm, late summer afternoon challenges the belief in human cognitive superiority.

So feigning a calm demeanor, I suggested to my gravely endangered children that we backpedal quickly and quietly out of this gaping enclosure of ice and satisfy our passions instead by throwing rocks or pebbles into the cave. Maybe even watch parts of it shudder and collapse while standing a safe distance away and—most importantly—on the outside.

As we tiptoed out, Joeline let out an audible sigh of relief and gave me a furtive, little hug, letting me know I narrowly escaped a stint in the dog house—even so, it would have been far better than being crushed in a collapsed ice house.

In my thirst for adventure, I tended to downplay the risks. But over time, as my kids got more involved, I slowly got better at choosing safer options—even at the expense of once-in-a-lifetime thrills. There was no better example of this than our trip to Colorado two years earlier.

🐾　🐾　🐾

My family and I had just finished cleaning up after our hot dog and macaroni and cheese dinner. In a rare moment of peace and quiet, all of us sat around the campfire, overlooking Turquoise Lake. Mount Elbert and Mount Massive loomed in the background. As I stared in awe at the summit of Mount Elbert, the highest peak in the North American Rocky Mountains, I envisioned standing atop its majestic slopes with the two older girls, hands in the air, basking in the glory of a successful ascent.

I shared this with Julie and Grace and threw in a little marketing mumbo jumbo, trying to persuade them to join me for such an adventure. Mollie went into convulsions. There would be no hiking or exploring or any exciting activity at all that didn't include her. Her pleading eventually wore me down, but when Max tried the same tactic, I had to draw the line.

All three girls agreed to come with me, obviously not knowing what would be involved. But Joeline knew, and she wasn't eager to sanction this whole idea of mine, especially after I mentioned that we would have to depart no later than six in the morning to have any chance of summiting before the afternoon thunderstorms.

Joeline insisted that rising before dawn was simply too far from our norm and would leave everyone cranky and exhausted all day. While this was inarguably true, it seemed like a minor issue compared to dying in a thunderstorm at thirteen thousand feet.

She agreed to an eight o'clock departure, reducing our chances of reaching the summit. It wasn't that likely we'd all make it to the top anyway, even if we left at six. While the trail isn't terribly long at five miles, it climbs almost five thousand feet—an arduous ascent. Plus, we were all flatlanders, unaccustomed to the thin air. But just having a go at the mountain would still be a great experience.

And what if we did make it, against all odds? The kids would have a lifelong memory—and so would I. But first I had to agree to a bunch of additional motherly conditions, all of which made complete sense, and finally Joeline okayed the expedition.

We got our gear ready for the next day, and the girls put together peanut butter and jelly sandwiches, taking great pains to pack them up nice and neat in plastic baggies.

"Sorry, ladies," I said. "It's impossible to keep sandwiches from getting smooshed on a hike. So just stuff them in your fanny packs and let's get to bed."

By two o'clock the next afternoon, to my total amazement, the four of us had managed to clamber up the mountain to well over thirteen thousand feet. We were less than fifteen hundred feet of elevation, or roughly an hour's climb, from the summit.

The trail was a killer, probably the steepest one I'd climbed since doing the north rim of the Grand Canyon. At one of our increasingly frequent rest stops, all three girls morphed into lifeless figures strewn across the rocks. I would have joined them, but there's something about rock surfaces that grinds me. Our sandwiches and trail mix had long since been eaten, and most of the water in our four canteens was gone, as was every bit of energy in the four bodies that had consumed it.

Hikers possessing good judgment and discipline were now descending from the pinnacle and could readily see we were drained.

"You're almost there," they said.

"Just another hour or so."

"You won't believe the view."

"Tough it out. You'll be glad you did."

"Look, you can see the peak right there."

Yes, you could see it. But was it *the* peak? Or just another in a series of peaks? How many times had we spent our last ounce of energy to reach some peak, only to discover it was another "false top," as the kids grew to call them?

The girls would probably never climb that high again in their lives, nor would I. We had expended so much energy to get so close—just a little more was required. The prospect of coming away unfulfilled was gut-wrenching. But the prospect of this being the end of our lives was more wrenching.

My biggest concern was potential thunderstorms, generally arriving mid- to late-afternoon. Like, say, two o'clock. Just the evening before, from our campsite, we had watched spellbound as dark clouds rolled up from the valley and over Mount Elbert, completely enveloping the massif in some violent precipitation. While this provides beautiful scenery to those in the campgrounds, it generally provides pure misery to those on the trail—and sometimes more than misery. The mountains are riddled with bad decisions.

The thrill of reaching the top can be addictive, as can so many of the short- or long-term goals we set for ourselves, or for others. The sky at this point didn't look threatening. But we were climbing up the north slope of the mountain and couldn't see the oncoming weather, typically blowing in from the southwest. The little devil on my right shoulder poked me with his pitchfork, urging me upward, but the haloed angel on my left warned of lightning bolts and blizzards, thunderclaps, and treacherous rain.

I usually give in to these temptations, but in a rare moment of caution and sanity, common sense won out. I told the girls we would finish our rest and then head back down.

Their consensus response was a listless "Okay, fine."

"Really? You don't want to go to the top?"

They all shook their heads. "Not really." Even Mollie joined in, having probably expended too much energy getting herself included on this expedition.

We were well above all the surrounding peaks, except for lumbering Mount Massive, about five miles to the north, approximately twelve feet shorter than Elbert. This small height difference, a difficult thing to measure in the "olden days," proved significant and caused great controversy. A dedicated group of proponents felt strongly that Massive deserved recognition as the highest point in Colorado because, as the name suggests, it is a far larger expanse of rock.

One afternoon these proponents hiked to the summit, gathered up thousands of rocks, and piled them as high as they could to increase its height. Elbert proponents, in turn, scrambled to the top of Massive and toppled the pile. The controversy continued until more accurate measurements finally proved Mount Elbert the winner.

Shortly after the four of us pointed our sneakers back down the mountain, the reverberations of thunder shook the slopes and storm clouds tumbled over the cliffs above us. It was a bittersweet pill to have abandoned our climb, but we were dry and intact, and most importantly, we'd be able to hike mountainous peaks again. I could tell from the girls' invigorated gait and enlivened dispositions that they didn't care about getting all the way to the top—and probably wouldn't even remember scaling the mountain.

And now I suspected that they wouldn't remember abandoning the ice cave either—that is, if they'd even remember entering it at all.

8.

the firing squad

Max and me freezing on Athabasca Glacier, Alberta, Canada.

Over coffee on Monday morning, Joeline and I agreed that we
should leave Jasper earlier than planned and head south. Originally, we intended to spend more time there, maybe four or five days,
to experience everything the gorgeous location offered. But we had
probably experienced it all, or at least enough of it, and we were ready
to begin our migration down the Icefields Parkway.

On previous trips, we had spent close to two hours every day just
breaking and pitching camp. So this time, we would set up camp only
three times—near Jasper and Banff and in Glacier National Park—
staying in each location for four or five days each.

From what we had seen of the crowds, we were taking a big risk
by heading out for a day's activity first and then looking for a camp-

site late in the afternoon. But this being a Monday, I was hoping it might be different.

We departed down Icefields Parkway, the famed 140-mile stretch of pristine highway that links Jasper to Lake Louise and provides some of the most breathtaking views anywhere: "tranquil waterfalls," "jagged rock spires," and more than a hundred "ancient glaciers"—so described in all the travel guides.

Now, I understand about tranquil waterfalls and jagged rock spires, but "ancient" glaciers? What glacier *isn't* ancient? "Hey, honey, lookie over there, on that mountain top. I think I see a brand-new glacier forming! Don't remember seeing that yesterday when I drove by."

We were about to discover firsthand the difference between the Canadian Rockies and the American Rockies we had visited two years before—that is, the Canadian Rockies are sharp and jagged, and between the mountains are wide, glacier-carved valleys, whereas the American Rockies are round, and between the mountains are narrow, river-carved valleys.

About halfway between Jasper and Banff, right along the parkway, lies the Columbia Icefield, home to the Athabasca Glacier, a spectacle we had been advised by multiple parties not to miss. Of course, you really can't miss it. The glacier "flows" from the mountain tops all along the west side of the valley, cascading down to within a few hundred yards of the highway.

We pulled off the parkway and into the lot and approached the ticket counter. Nothing was cheap in this part of the world, we found out repeatedly, especially when multiplied by seven. Today, it would cost a family our size $600 for the "glacier adventure." Other packages were also available, for which the prices only skyrocketed.

But there are very few glaciers in North Carolina, especially ancient ones, so we had to go on some type of adventure. Joeline and I settled for the basic package, departing on the noon Ice Explorer, with the option to return at our leisure on any down bound ride.

We hopped on a shuttle that drove us to the edge of the glacier, where we boarded a monster all-terrain vehicle that would haul us up and out onto the glacier. As we began moving, a muffled, crackling recorded voice came over the speakers. "The Columbia Icefield, located astride the Continental Divide, is one of the largest non-polar icefields, with a depth of twelve hundred feet. It formed during the Great Glaciation, long before Homo sapiens roamed the earth. It's been estimated that some of the snow, or ice, that works its way out at the bottom of the glacier may have fallen from the clouds around the year 1000 AD."

Now that would qualify as "ancient."

The kids stepped out onto the immense span of ice and snow spawning out in every direction and surrounded by snowcapped mountains—a surreal world of wonder and shock. Only with focused vigilance and caution did they dare move their feet on this exotic surface. It was like gliding across a choppy sea that had frozen during a storm. Bits of smooth, slippery ice were interspersed with thick chunks. There were mint-green streamlets everywhere, trickling over and under and through the ice and then disappearing into sink holes.

The tour guide stood near the Explorer talking into her microphone, mumbling something we couldn't understand. Mollie slid into me and grabbed my arm.

"This is really cool, Dad. I feel like I'm walking on water. But the ice seems to be melting. It's kinda scary."

It sure is, I thought. *This could all collapse and we'd all be dead and frozen in seconds.* I put my arm around Mollie and kept my thoughts to myself.

Joeline held a firm grip on Max's safety strap, trying to avert him from sinking into a frigid hole and into the arctic abyss below. Luckily for her, he was way more interested in the mammoth truck tires on the Ice Explorer than in the slow-moving icefield we had just paid a fortune to ascend.

The guides had assured us that the water pooled up in the puddles around us was some of the purest on earth and encouraged us to fill our hands or bottles. Grace dropped to her knees excitedly and slurped up a handful of the pristine glacial runoff. She looked up, furrowing her eyebrows. "This tastes just like the water in Charlotte. And now I can't feel my fingers."

Recalling our overriding objective to get a campsite for the next few days, I grudgingly shuffled everyone onto a departing vehicle, taking us back to the visitor center slightly ahead of our schedule.

I asked one of the attendants at the center about the availability of campgrounds down the parkway. "You'll find several campgrounds ahead, within fifty to sixty miles. If you take off right now, you should be able to snag a spot somewhere, no problem."

I clenched the steering wheel tightly the entire way, hopeful but skeptical. I hated having to set up camp in a crappy site or, even worse, next to the crapper. The latrine-side sites were usually the last to be claimed. No one wants to gaze into a campfire nestled in the wafting breeze from the outhouse.

Aside from being an eyesore, the bathrooms are home to a variety of bugs that go about their business as you go about yours. Guys can generally make their way into a latrine, take care of their needs, and exit without even noticing the spiders. Ladies, on the other hand, can tell you not only the number of spiders occupying the space, but also their location, size, and color, as well as the direction they're moving in—more specifically, whether they are approaching or retreating. They're never retreating.

Just the thought of being anywhere close to an arachnid sanctuary sent most of my family into webs of despair. Julie and Angela were the most disturbed, but somehow, they eventually learned how to enter and exit the latrine with only the pads of their toes coming into contact with any surfaces.

Grace was the exception, displaying very little fear. She liked to play with the roly-polies (this is not the actual scientific name for the species—I think it is rolus polus latrinae) and didn't mind sharing her bathroom space with them. In fact, I think they provided her with some light entertainment. The bugs didn't bother me anywhere near as much as the foul odor emanating from the communal commode. Bathroom proximity, I soon discovered, wasn't going to be an issue for us on that particular night. And that is because there were no open sites for sixty miles. Instead, we headed for the designated primitive overflow area near one of the campgrounds and easily secured a decent spot. The good news: we weren't anywhere near a bathroom. The bad news: there was no bathroom to be anywhere near to. "Primitive" means no bathrooms or water or electricity or any modern comforts. Just a little clearing. But that was okay. We would manage.

The only real nuisance was an overly friendly, mildly detached gentleman, looking endlessly for his dog, Willy. After his third time around the grounds, we began to realize that there probably was no Willy. Probably never had been. The man seemed harmless, but he wandered the campground for hours, calling, "Hey, Willy. Come here, boy." It gave us the willies.

We were in something of a bowl area surrounded by mountains on all sides, right next to a small lake. Since there was no running water around, this location would probably be a one-nighter, but a beautiful one it would be.

We cooked up some sausages and then went to the lake to do a little faux fishing—that's when you cast your line into the water without any bait secured to the hook to avoid catching anything you would then have to extract from the hook. The technique is generally more effective with younger children and sometimes with teenage girls who share your lack of excitement over detaching slimy creatures from deadly barbed hooks.

After bedding down the kids, Joeline and I sat by the campfire, looking out at the lake with the dim reflection of the moonlit mountains floating on the surface. We were startled from our little retreat by a figure lurking in the distance. The search for Willy might be resuming. Instead, a ranger wandered into the firelight.

"Good evening, folks." he said. "Looks like a nice, hot fire you got going there."

I'm sorry, but I couldn't help thinking, *No, actually, this here's a cold fire we got going.*

"Just want to remind y'all," he said. "Be sure to soak it out before going to bed. We've had extremely dry conditions these past few weeks, and late burning fires can be really dangerous out here."

I have always preferred to let the campfire die out on its own, the crackle and spitting lulling me to sleep. Reluctantly, we told him we'd comply, and he disappeared back into the darkness.

"It's gonna be pitch black without the fire," Joeline said. "I sure wish we had some oil for those lanterns."

"Yep, I know. On the top of my list. Right above the camera batteries."

As we were dousing the hot fire with some wet water, she said, "You know, this campsite didn't turn out all that bad. I'm kinda glad we ended up here."

"Me too."

Yes, we had lucked out. When we ended up at a remote location during my Wild West trip, we didn't fare as well—although it wasn't exactly a "designated" camping area.

The five of us guys had pulled out of Las Vegas one evening after a short stay in Sin City, setting our sights on the coastal town of San Diego. It would be the first encounter with an ocean for several of us. It's roughly a six-hour journey between these two cities, but none of us savants had the foresight to do the math. As a result, we didn't start seeing exits for San Diego until well past midnight.

We took the first one and then searched for someplace secluded, yet adequately spacious for our sleeping gear. Pretty much collectively brain dead at this point, we spied a sign for Miramar College, which one of us geniuses interpreted to be a private girls' college.

We sneaked around back and drove across a large open field to the end of campus. Nobody would see us back there, and we'd vacate early in the morning, as soon as someone woke up. We spread our gear out on the grass in less than five minutes and fell sound asleep soon after.

Waking up wasn't a problem. At five o'clock or so, the sounds of rapid machine gunfire blasted us into consciousness. What the hell? We flailed around, running into one another, halfway stuck in our sleeping bags, some in our boxers, others without (Mel), screaming and yelling at ourselves, terrified. About fifty yards to our right, a dozen neatly uniformed sharpshooters were firing away at targets—which we presumed were us, but were actually human-shaped cutouts positioned about fifty yards to our left. The projectiles were flying no more than ten feet from our shell-shocked faces and continued for a few more minutes until the marksmen fell over, exhausted from laughter.

No one in the entire history of camping has ever broken out of a site faster.

Speeding out of the battleground, we passed the sign out front and discovered that our "genius" had misread it. We had just spent the night at the San Diego Regional Public Safety Training Institute at Miramar College. Nothing on that sign could have remotely suggested the existence of a girls' college. We had camped out on the firing range of a police academy. The cadets had more fun that morning than they'd had in a long time. Instead of using dummy targets, they got to use real dummies as targets.

I sat with my beautiful wife and watched the dying fire for another few minutes to make sure every last ember was out. We didn't want to be responsible for burning down the park.

Joeline retreated to the comfort of Big Blue. Before joining her, I took stock of our surroundings. An expansive night sky filled with tiny stars, a mountain brook gurgling nearby, and snowcapped mountains in the distance. I was actually sorry we couldn't stay another night. But we were determined to get to a campground early enough the next day to have our choice of spots, hopefully even find a campsite close to a river, with flushing toilets and hot showers—as long as they were an acceptable distance from our tent.

9.

riding the kicking horse

View of Kicking Horse River from our campsite.

The deep crimson of early dawn peered over the mountains to the east and slowly grew into a band of pink and then full yellow rays, spilling into the waiting sky. The rays swept down the gray cliffs behind us, soon lighting up the walls of our big blue tent.

I stretched out on my air mattress for several minutes, only a few paltry millimeters from the rocky earth below, soaking up the serenity of another beautiful morning filled with warm sunshine and tranquil birds. All five children slept peacefully.

I almost hated to wake them. Mainly because it required so much work. I could have rolled their sleeping bags over, pulled down the tent poles, and poured cold water all over them, but I still wouldn't have gotten the intended results.

Even so, it was critical for us to take off early to secure a campsite at our next stop. I rolled off my mattress, stood, and called out, "Wake up, you sleeping beauties. We have to pack and get down the road."

There was a lot of moaning and groaning, but the kids got busy. Surprisingly, Joeline was the one lagging behind. She kept going from one bag to the next, frantically looking for something. Her shoulders slumped. "Marty, I'm totally out of clean underwear. I can't believe I didn't pack more. Now I have to recycle."

"Do what?"

"Turn a dirty pair inside out, and just hope to God nobody sees them. My mother would have a fit if she knew I was leaving the tent in dirty underwear."

I've never understood this rule, passed down by generations of mothers. My father never once warned me not to leave the house without changing my boxers. He simply asked me to leave.

"Whatever works. We'll find a way to do some laundry in a day or two."

As usual, we were the first campers up and at it, but given how long our kids took to pack—and the adults to reverse their undergarments—we were the last to finally pull out. All the other vacationers were probably headed to the same campground we were, even though we didn't know precisely where we were going.

Based on all the guide books and brochures, I thought we'd have the most success at the low-density camping locations. So that ruled out the general Lake Louise/Banff area. We would be better off driving toward Yoho National Park, portentously named after the Cree expression meaning "awe and wonder."

It took about half an hour to reach the Trans-Canada Highway, and the traffic diminished significantly as we veered off to the right in a westerly direction. When we approached the Canadian Pacific Railway's dueling Spiral Tunnels, I was tempted to pull over to check out the nominee for one of the seven wonders of the Canadian world. But I resisted, hoping to return to enjoy it after securing a beautiful campsite.

Kicking Horse was the first significant-sized campground on the horizon, and unbelievably, there was no FULL/COMPLET sign anywhere. We must have missed it, but I wasn't doubling back to check. We scrambled through the park entrance and hurried into the line at the registration booth.

It was only nine o'clock, but even with all the hustling, we were fourth in line. The tension mounted. Would there be more than three sites available this early? Would they be next to the bathroom? Would there be *any* bathrooms?

The campers moved through the line briskly, and soon, it was our turn. The plump ranger smiled and nodded hello. "Good morning," she said in a spirited tone. "How can I help you?"

I peered into the ranger's eyes, looking for any telltale sign of FULL/COMPLET.

"Good morning to you, ma'am." I glanced at her name tag. "Ranger Murray. We're just hoping to get a nice campsite." I paused. "Next to the river, if that's possible?"

Camping next to streams had become our wilderness protocol. Fresh mountain brooks provided hours of entertainment for the kids and added a panoramic backdrop to our outdoor experience. Best of all, the gentle water rippling by serenaded me to sleep, fulfilling some basic primal need I didn't even know I had.

I held my breath as she flipped through some papers and then looked up. "Here we go. Site forty-two. Right next to the river."

"Perfect! Thank you."

I couldn't believe our luck.

"Now, I'm not sure what you folks have planned for the next few days, but I always recommend to everyone to check out Emerald Lake. It's Yoho's largest lake and famous for its deep green-colored water. It's just beautiful. They also offer canoe rides throughout the day. Looks like you have a few kids in there with you—they all might enjoy that."

"I'll put that at the top of our agenda for tomorrow. Thanks for the suggestion."

As I started to pull away, Grace, obsessed with horses since her youngest days, stuck her head out the window. "Are there horses here? Is that why they call it Kicking Horse Campground?"

"Afraid not." The ranger handed her a map. "Check out the back. It has some history of the area."

Grace eagerly scanned it. "Get this," she said. "Apparently, some explorer named James Hector was trying to rescue a horse from the river when another horse kicked him in the chest and knocked him unconscious. The guys with him thought he was dead, so they dug a grave, and just as they were about to toss him in, he regained consciousness! So they named the river the Kicking Horse and then named the campground after the river."

What a ridiculous name. If a horse kicked me unconscious and I was nearly buried alive, we'd be pitching our tent at Dead Horse Campground.

The campsite was even nicer than I imagined. It was out in the open, except for a low but thick semicircle of bushes that provided total privacy from the passing traffic. We had an amazing view of the surrounding mountains and the river was only a hundred feet away. We delayed setting up camp and made a beeline to play in the water.

I had heard that the Kicking Horse was glacier-fed, but I wasn't expecting a torrent tearing its way through the mountain valley. Down a short but steep, rocky embankment, the river looked to be only a few feet deep on average and probably forty feet across, but its frigid waters flowed swiftly and violently past. I'd have to establish some stringent usage guidelines. For the time being, our little pioneers were rolling some of the larger rocks into the water's edge, building some makeshift dams close to shore. They added some shrubbery and sticks for good measure.

Back up on higher ground, I discovered that our site had only one level area large enough to accommodate the circumference of our seven-person tent. But dead center in that spot was a gnarly chunk of timber lodged firmly in the ground. It was protruding just enough to present a serious obstacle to anyone interested in getting any sleep. It would have to be extracted.

I pounded on it with our tent peg hammer a few times to loosen it up, but with little luck. Then I dug around it with our Boy Scout shovel and blasted away at it with our firewood ax. After roughly fifteen minutes of full-frontal assault, I was able to pry the stubborn log from its tomb. In a rush of exhilaration, I heaved it mightily toward the river, only to notice thousands of tiny red specks flying off the log. What the hell were those? I peered down into the hole. Holy Christ! Three hundred million enraged red ants were coming after me in full force, none too thrilled with what I had just done to their living quarters.

I'd have to deal with these pests the same way I dealt with the hornet nests back home in North Carolina—dousing them with gasoline. We hadn't used our Coleman stove yet, so we had plenty of fuel available. I carefully poured some of it around and into the hole where the log had been.

But it didn't slow the ants down one bit—they became even more frantic and excited. They actually seemed to be feeding off the gas and its fumes. Imagine being invigorated by the immersion into and ingestion of gasoline. Reminded me of my college days.

I thought for a second, and clearly not any longer than that, before launching my final offensive—torching the community. I lit a match.

It seemed like a good idea, but when the searing fireball, infused with furious, flaming red ants, blasted skyward, nearly taking my few remaining locks with it, I realized I had shortchanged the planning cycle. Thank God I wasn't completely hunched over the hole when I flung the match.

The ranger's words from the previous night sprang to mind: "hot fire," "extremely dry conditions," "really dangerous." Forest fires were raging in British Columbia, Alberta, Washington, Oregon, and Montana. And here I was pouring gasoline all over the ground and blithely torching it. This might be a little tricky to explain to the judge. "You see, Your Honor, there were millions of red ants hogging up the only flat space in our campsite. I had no choice but to nuke 'em. It never occurred to me I could burn down the entire province."

Now fully crazed and yelling at myself, I began kicking sand and dirt into the ant hole, dancing around like a maniac. Flames continued to shoot out of the ground.

"Dad, Dad!" Julie shouted, and shoved a bucket at me. "Mom told us to pump some water for you."

"You're a lifesaver! Get more."

I doused the hole—flooding most of our campsite along with it—extinguishing the fire and in turn drowning most of the ants.

I filled the hole with gravel, let it smolder for a few moments, and then covered it with sand and dirt and leaves to help absorb the deluge. After allowing some drying time, we spread a few large pieces of tarp on the ground and set about pitching our tent over the mass grave.

It turned out we were within a few miles of one of the highest waterfalls in Canada—Takakkaw Falls. We loaded up the kids and set out to explore. What a beautiful, exciting drive! Well, I classified it as exciting, but Joeline classified it as horrifying.

Whenever I traverse narrow, winding mountain roads, like those in Yoho National Park, I'm tempted to hug the edge of the pavement, enjoying the view straight out into thin air and down to sharp rocks below. I've even been known to bellow a hearty "Yeehaw!" The kids enjoyed it too, having absolutely no understanding or awareness of their mortality.

As we approached the falls, an unusual hush overtook the van. Eyeballs bulged and jaws hung agape as we were all simultaneously struck by the majesty and grandeur of the canyon. The silence in the car was almost as magnificent as the scenery. We had driven a little way from the interstate, and the place was surprisingly devoid of the usual hordes we'd been experiencing. Especially surprising, considering how well the Cree word *takakkaw*—meaning "magnificent"—described this site.

The kids tumbled out of the car and sped off toward the falls. "Hey!" I called out. "Hold on, you clowns. Mom's getting lunch ready." And then I quickly added, "With cookies."

Joeline was spreading out the main course of peanut butter and jelly sandwiches on a picnic table with a view of the falls. "Those cookies are for s'mores, you know, so you'd better think of something else to bribe them with."

"Uh, yeah, hadn't thought about that. Do we still have some doughnuts left over from Jasper? That'll probably keep 'em quiet."

"They're stale."

"They're doughnuts. The kids will never notice."

Not only did they fail to notice, but after their sandwiches had disappeared, they inhaled the pastries without the slightest interruption to their talking.

As Angela was wiping the last globs of jelly filling from her lips, she snuggled up to Joeline. "Mommy, where does all the water go?"

An astute observation on her part. Despite the voluminous flow over the top, the water did seem to dissipate into a thick, floating mist towards the bottom of its twelve-hundred-foot plunge. Twelve hundred feet—higher than the Empire State Building.

"Why don't we all hike over there and find out where the water goes?" Joeline said.

Grace took the lead as we strung out in a line, leaning into the moist breeze. She called back to us, "When I look up, I get so much water in my eyes I can't see where I'm going."

Eventually we had to abandon the direct approach altogether and hike up onto the rocks on the uphill side of the falls to avoid being blinded and then blasted off into the whirlwind below. After a few more steps upward, Joeline reached out and grabbed my arm from behind. "Martin, should we really be doing this? I know they're having a great time, but someone's going to get hurt."

I stopped immediately and surveyed our situation. Sure enough, too much looking down had allowed us to proceed into dangerous territory. I yelled out to the kids, "Let's just stop here and soak in this waterfall for a couple of minutes. Then we'll turn back."

The only dissident was Max. "Can't we keep going? I want to go where the water slams into the boulders."

"We could, Max, but I think we would all die."

He picked up a small rock and hurled it at the falls in disappointment and then lost his balance, slipped, and landed on his rear end. It was a blessed event, scaring the crap out of him enough to make him stop resisting our upcoming retreat.

The hurricane winds covered us with tiny droplets of freezing cold water. Straining to remain vertical, we lingered there, mesmerized, for several minutes. Or was it several hours? Time seemed to stand still.

Joeline bent down, wiped the droplets from Angela's face, and showed them to her. "This is where all the water goes," she said.

Angela glanced down at her mom's hand and then up at her face. "Oh."

At six years old, Angela was honing the art of understatement.

"Okay, folks," I said, "time to turn around."

We resumed our lineup, all holding hands, and picked our way slowly through the jagged boulders, the wet wind pounding at our backs instead of at our faces. Everyone could look up and down, making our safe return much more likely. I carried Max most of the way, a lot easier and safer than directing him.

We slid on feet and fannies a few times, arriving somewhat disheveled and a little worn at the parking lot.

It was now late afternoon. What day was it? I'd completely lost track. We arrived on Friday. No, Thursday . . . Oh crap, it was already Tuesday! Despite my planning, with all the distractions, I hadn't checked in with Seth once. My entire territory could have gone up in smoke and taken my job with it.

"Joel, I'm going to run us back down to the ranger station. I need to call the office."

It took about fifteen minutes to drive down to the campground and about five seconds for the ranger, a guy this time, to tell me I couldn't tie up his phone.

"Sorry, sir. Too much going on this afternoon. You can use the pay phone at the Yoho Park visitor center in Field. Just across the river."

Three minutes later, we arrived in Field, population two hundred, and located the visitor center right away. It was the only building on the other side of the river, not to mention one of the only buildings in the whole town.

The young guide on duty, Amanda, shook her head. No, they didn't have a pay phone. "But there's one across the river at the first intersection."

So the ranger was just trying to get rid of me. Unbelievable.

I scanned the room, taking in the maps and brochures. "Do you have any activities here for a family of seven?"

Like Ranger Murray that morning, Amanda recommended the canoe trip around Emerald Lake. "But your parent-to-kid ratio is too low," she said. "You'll need three canoes and you have to have an adult in each one. I'd be happy to join you tomorrow and take one of the kids in my canoe."

"I can't turn that offer down!" I said. "What time do we set sail?"

"At ten. We'll be the first tour out. That way I'll be free to go with you."

"Excellent! See you then."

When I told Joeline, she said, "This means we'll need to be up and at 'em no later than eight-thirty to get there on time."

An eight-thirty arousal might not seem like that big a deal, but we were a slow-moving group in the morning. Really. Slow.

Back across the river, I finally found the pay phone. I pulled out my MCI calling card, relieved that I had remembered to bring it with me. It was late on the East Coast, but Seth would still be there. He never went home.

"Marty! How the hell are you? Everything okay? I was wondering if you were going to call."

"Things have been hectic, and it's tricky finding pay phones around here. How's everything going?"

"I have everything under control. Just the usual shit."

"Yeah, that's exactly what I'm afraid of. The 'usual shit' means there are explosions all over the place."

"Seriously, I've been keeping tabs on everybody. We're good here."

But things were never "good," only bad in varying degrees—sorta bad, real bad, awful bad, disastrous bad.

"All right," I said, letting out a long exhale. "I'll check back in on Friday."

Oh God, I needed to find a new job.

At the campsite, we ventured down to the river to see if any of our dams had held up. To our utter astonishment, one not only held up, but had been reinforced with enough debris to cause the river to roar and foam through the narrowed passage. We stayed back, skipping in the required rocks and stones.

At dusk, everyone made their way to the showers in flip-flops. One advantage to camping in a cooler climate is less sweating. But in the record heat, certain members of the group were ripe for a hose down, myself included.

For dinner, Joeline roasted up hickory-smoked spaghetti. Max taught Angela how to burn a sausage beyond recognition and then smother it in ketchup to hide the taste of charcoal. The older girls sat at the picnic table laughing and laying out graham crackers and marshmallows and devouring the chocolate squares.

I leaned comfortably against the picnic table, my feet stretched out in front of me, soaking up the sounds of my family. This was exactly what I had been looking forward to.

After Joeline got our happy campers all sacked out for the night in their sleeping bags and zipped up the tent windows, she came outside and handed me a flashlight. "Let's go for a little walk."

"I think we've finally escaped the crowds," I said, reaching for her hand. "Are you having a good time?"

"I'm having a great time, but . . . Marty, we might have a problem." She sounded way too serious.

"When I went to the water pumps before dinner, I noticed that one of them was labeled 'non-potable.'"

"Uh-huh." Waiting for the punch line.

"Are you listening to me? You know that means 'don't drink,' right?"

"Sure, I know that"—actually, I wasn't completely sure if I knew that—"but do the kids?"

"I doubt it. They filled the jugs from both pumps. So some of us probably drank the unsanitary stuff. This is what I get for all my preaching about drinking plenty of water."

"Everyone seems fine so far. Don't blame yourself. Drinking lots of water is usually a good thing."

"Yeah, we might be okay now, but what about in a couple of days? Can you imagine five kids vomiting in the tent or having explosive diarrhea out in the woods? Or in a canoe in the middle of a lake?" Joeline looked at me with horror. "Maybe we shouldn't go tomorrow."

Well, God *damn* it. Wasn't that just perfect. Now that we could finally start relaxing, this happened. I stopped walking, trying to alter my attitude.

"I think you can stop worrying, Joel. If the water was that bad, would they have put it so close to the drinking water?"

"That's a good point."

"The kids are having fun. And the canoe ride is going to be wonderful."

"You think we should still go?"

"I do." I tired to ignore my ghastly visions of the kids spewing overboard.

"You're right. Maybe nothing will come of it. And I was really looking forward to being out on the water. Sounds like Emerald Lake is gorgeous."

Back at our site, she wrapped her arms around me and smiled. "I love you."

"I love you too."

I leaned in to kiss her when a rustling came from the circle of bushes. My head swung around and my heart rate shot up. "Didn't the ranger say something about a momma bear and her two cubs hanging around the grounds?" Bears had become way too real for me.

It took us two and a half seconds to get inside our bear-proof tent. Tents are bear-proof in much the same way that blankets are monster-proof.

We huddled together on my air mattress, still underinflated, adding substantially to our serious lack of comfort. Barely breathing, we peered into the darkness. Joeline dug her fingernails through my plaid shirt and into my side. "I can still hear them out there," she whispered.

The last time this happened I was in a tent by myself. That's right. I'd been in this predicament before.

About twenty-five years earlier, after graduating from high school, three buddies and I took a camping and canoeing trip through the Algonquin Provincial Park in Ontario. The day we arrived, I came down with the flu, so after several hours of canoeing through some wild, dense marshlands, I immediately pitched my tent and burrowed into my sleeping bag.

Drifting in and out of consciousness, I desperately tried to get some rest while my three companions horsed around outside. With great relief, I finally heard them pack up some gear and wander away from the campsite.

I dozed off for a while, only to be awakened too soon by their raucous laughter. It was impossible to ignore them, especially when they kept calling to me in a hilarious medley, "Hey, Marty. Be careful of those bears swiping away at your tent."

In my debased condition, I was in no mood for their stupid antics. I tried to ignore them and go back to sleep. But then they started rustling my tent, so much so I thought they might rip it to shreds. I sprang up and glared at the entrance, my head throbbing.

Their snickering continued, their voices coming from several paces off in the distance. Wait a second. How could that be? If those bastards were that far away, who—or what—was rustling my tent? I unzipped the flap just enough to come face-to-snout with a pair of bear cubs staring back at me. It's not possible that they were more terrified than I was, but in impressive unison, they jumped up and scampered away into the woods.

Now, I was no zoologist, but I knew enough to know that where there were baby bears, there was a momma bear. And maybe a daddy bear and sisters and cousins and aunts. The best place for me right then was in our vehicle. I almost did myself permanent damage getting out of that tent. But as I stood there, sweating and feeling quite unhinged, it hit me. We didn't have a vehicle. All we had were canoes. A canoe is a bit like a serving platter to a hungry bear.

It was time for a fast, deeply earnest Hail Mary. *Mother, most merciful, please help us . . . but mainly me!*

Apparently, she heard me. We saw no more signs of the cubs or their momma or any other relatives. The whole thing was more humorous than anything—my friends sure busted a gut—and it instilled in me a lifelong distinct and profound dread for the kings of the forest. Sorry, Mr. Lion. Until a lion cub swipes away at my tent, bears will continue to be my chief nemesis.

At eighteen years old, I learned my first basic lesson in wilderness awareness: bears really do live (as well as shit) in the woods.

Inside Big Blue, I pulled Joeline closer. Could the bears smell us? Should we be putting an evacuation plan in place? Forget contaminated water and explosive diarrhea. Would we survive through the night? Through the next five minutes? Could we all make it to the van? God, was it unlocked? Where were the keys?

Time for another Hail Mary.

10.

angels in the outfield

Canoe shack on Emerald Lake.

Forty years of rising at the crack of dawn every Sunday to attend mass must have paid off. The Blessed Mother had kept the bears away from our tent. Either that or all the ruckus had been coming from two rowdy raccoons. Everything sounds bigger in the woods.

With some genial maternal coaxing, we managed to get underway early on Wednesday. Seven bowls of Frosted Mini-Wheats summarily consumed, we were pulling away from our campsite when I noticed we had left the westerly tent windows wide open. "I better zip back and zip up the flaps."

Joeline rolled down her window. "Don't worry about it. We'll only be gone a couple of hours." She stuck her hand outside. "Besides, it hasn't rained here in two months."

I shot a curious glance her way. How was it that I was worried about something and she wasn't? But Joeline's approach would definitely be easier. "You're right. And it wouldn't hurt to let everything air out a bit. Some of our gear is getting pretty musty."

I steered the van toward the campground exit, one hand on the wheel, the other holding a map. No doubt, we could have executed these two duties more effectively if we had split them between pilot and copilot. But history had demonstrated that when Joeline was the navigator, within minutes, one of our younger members would ask, "Mom, are we lost yet?"

About six miles up the access road, we arrived at Emerald Lake, and I parked in the shade. Through the trees, I could see the early morning light shimmering on the water. We couldn't have asked for more spectacular weather. "I'll run over and check in at the canoe hut. Get your stuff together so we can go as soon as I get back."

"I need to use the bathroom first," Joeline said.

"Didn't you go before we left?" I asked.

"Yes, but there's one right there, and we're going to be in a canoe for two hours, so I want to be on empty when we set sail."

"I have to go too," Julie said, hopping out of the van. "Don't worry. We'll be quick."

How do you get emptier than empty? And why do women have to travel in pairs to use the facilities? I popped my head into the van. "Anyone else have to go?" Blank stares. "Good. Wait here for your mother and Julie. I'll only be a minute. Put on some sunscreen while I'm gone."

As I walked down toward the canoes, the full expanse of Emerald Lake came into view. My God, it was beautiful. Surrounded by imposing peaks of sheer mountain limestone, the water sparkled like the gemstone it was named for.

At the shack, Amanda was standing in the doorway, a cup of coffee in her hand. "Good morning, Mr. Ohlhaut! I'm glad you guys made it. It's a perfect day to be out on the water."

"Couldn't agree more. I wanted to get us all checked in. The kids are getting their stuff together and using the bathroom."

"No problem. We've got plenty of time and several canoes available. We can figure out who's riding with who when you're ready to go. While you're down here, why don't you pick out life jackets for everyone from that pile over there?"

I gathered up six right away, but couldn't find an extra-large. I was certainly not the biggest guy who had ever squeezed into a canoe, but I must have been the biggest one to paddle around Emerald Lake. I was clipping two jackets together when Amanda called over to me, "That's clever, but not necessary. We have some oversized ones in the back."

Oversized? Why not man-sized, or brawny-sized?

"Let me get one, and I'll bring all the stuff down to the canoes."

"Sounds like a plan. I'll round everyone up, and we'll meet you in a couple of minutes."

I jogged back to the van to gather the sailors. Surprisingly Julie and Joeline weren't there. They were taking uncharacteristically long for such a characteristically short procedure.

I looked up through the woods toward the ladies' restroom but couldn't see anyone. Where the heck did they go? I marched off to find them.

As I started up the hill, a tumultuous crash stopped me in my tracks. It was like something you might hear in a restaurant when some poor waiter drops a tray full of dishes—silverware clanging, glass shattering. The noise seemed to have come from behind the handicapped restroom in front of me, not the ladies' room up to the left. But now it was completely quiet. Had I heard a big accident from way off on the highway? Or maybe I had imagined the whole thing.

Still no sign of my wife or daughter. Then I heard Joeline's quivering voice. "It's bad. It's real bad."

She stumbled out from behind the handicapped facilities.

My heart nearly stopped. "Joeline!"

She was covered in blood. Her blouse, her shorts, her arms, her legs. Blood everywhere. Hunched over, she wobbled and struggled to stand.

Julie appeared behind her, screaming, "Dad!"

I raced to them and reached out to hold Joeline up, but Julie and I could only help her crumple to the ground. She had cuts all over her body and shards of glass stuck to her skin.

So much blood.

I looked over at Julie, not believing what I was seeing. "What happened?"

"Mom fell out the window!" she cried, her eyes wide with alarm.

"She what?"

"Someone was using the other bathroom . . . so we used the handicapped . . . she got locked inside and tried to climb out."

Julie cradled her mom's head in her lap. Joeline was amazingly calm, lying still, not thrashing about in hysterics as I would have been. Tears in her eyes, she whispered, "I'm sorry. I'm so sorry."

"Oh, honey, what for?" I jumped up, not waiting for an answer. "We need help." I bolted down to the canoe shack.

"Amanda, call an ambulance! My wife's had an accident!" Dashing out, I shouted over my shoulder, "Up near the parking lot. She's bleeding. It's bad!"

Back where Joeline was lying on the grass, a middle-aged Asian couple had appeared and were kneeling on either side of her, holding on to her leg. Who the hell were they? And what were they doing?

I got down on the ground and heard them talking softly to each other in a language I couldn't make out. The man looked up at me. "Your wife?" he asked. I nodded. He pointed to himself. "Doctor."

A doctor? Here, in the middle of nowhere?

They were wiping blood from Joeline's body with something I never would have thought of—maxi pads. Their backpack was stuffed with them.

But the blood kept coming.

My stomach twisted. I could lose her, right here, right now, this very morning. *Dear God, please don't let that happen.* I wanted to touch her, to hold her, but with all the blood and cuts and glass shards, I might make it worse.

"Joel, you know this guy's a doctor, right?"

She gave me a weak smile. "Yeah. The two of them just showed up. Must be my guardian angels."

"They probably are. They're going to help take care of you until the ambulance gets here." I glanced back and forth between the man and the woman. "Thank you," I managed to choke out.

The man bowed his head in response. Then he reached for a couple of pads and applied pressure to the long gash on Joeline's right bicep. It looked like a raw sausage that had been cut in half lengthwise, all the filling oozing out. I had never seen anything like it.

I felt dizzy and weak, my vision darkening around the edges. I swallowed hard and took several deep breaths. It was all I could do not to pass out.

Julie's face was very pale. Mine probably was too. Neither of us does well at the mere sight of blood, or a needle, or even talk of blood or a needle. She brushed tears away with the back of her hand as she picked small shards of glass off her mom.

Without saying a word, the doctor showed me how to massage the "sausage" back into Joeline's arm and gently close up the skin. Apparently, when lacerations are really, really deep, the stuff that is normally inside your body starts working its way out. I grabbed a pad to apply pressure. It took the entire width of my hand and then some to cover the gash.

"Joel, you've got a cut on your arm here. I'm just working to stop the bleeding."

"Where are the kids?" she asked, her voice full of panic. "They can't see me like this."

"It's okay, Mom," Julie said. "They're over by the van."

The doctor took Joeline's pulse and then put his hand on her forehead, most likely checking for signs of shock. The woman lifted the pad she had been pressing on a laceration on Joeline's thigh above her left knee, revealing an even bigger "sausage."

Oh God, how many were there?

I scanned her trembling body for more. Blood continued to gurgle from her many cuts. The ones on her right arm and left leg appeared to be the worst. I spotted a few others that might have been considered serious, but in this case, "serious" was taking on a more ominous meaning.

I studied the man and woman tending so meticulously to my wife—two complete strangers. They seemed somehow familiar, as if we had met before. The woman caught my eye and gave me a sympathetic smile.

By this time, a few hushed onlookers had gathered in the parking lot. The woman left Joeline's side and walked over to our other children, who had been watching this whole catastrophe play out in stunned silence. She crouched down and took Angela's hands in hers and then hugged Mollie and Grace and patted Max on his back.

Joeline was fading in and out, growing disturbingly quiet. The bleeding still hadn't stopped, but when someone mentioned using a tourniquet, she perked right up. "No way! Absolutely not."

"Don't worry, Joel, no tourniquets. I won't let anyone touch you except the doctor."

My head was pounding. Where the hell was the ambulance? Was one even on the way? We were way out in the Canadian wilderness. Did they even have emergency vehicles out here?

Another five minutes passed—seemed like an hour. I was about to hurry down and ask Amanda for an update when I heard a chorus of sirens approaching. An ambulance, accompanied by several park emergency vehicles, pulled up near us. Three paramedics piled out and swarmed around Joeline while a fourth one emerged with a gurney.

The cavalry had arrived in the nick of time—and not only for Joeline. Julie and I were about to keel over. Standing up, I said, "Let's let these guys do their job." I reached out to take Julie's hand but stopped when I saw how bloody mine were. I motioned us instead to a nearby bench.

We collapsed onto it. Undeterred by our medical ineptitude, we had performed our grim duties, aided by a mysterious force that sometimes creeps in, corrals the emotions, and helps people do what they otherwise couldn't. Julie had stayed so calm, performing like a battle-seasoned veteran. I couldn't have been prouder of my oldest daughter.

Wait! I had to thank the doctor and his wife who had also retreated when the emergency medical technicians had arrived. How would we have managed without them?

Not seeing them nearby, I got up and searched the immediate area and then glanced around the entire parking lot. No sight of them. Their backpack had been sitting in the grass, its unusual contents spilling out. It, too, was gone. The shore of the lake was empty. The causeway over to the lodge was deserted. None of this made sense. How could they be gone so quickly? Why hadn't they stayed around to do whatever it was that brought them here in the first place?

Just as mysteriously as they had appeared, they vanished.

We never saw them again.

The EMTs were still working on Joeline, so I hustled to the bathroom to figure out what had happened. From the far side of the small building, I could see the window in question high up on the wall, at least six feet above the ground. It was horizontally positioned, opened to the outside, and hinged on the bottom. The glass was shattered, although several large, blood-streaked fragments were stuck in the frame, which was still somehow connected to the wall.

How was Joeline able to slide her body out and over the frame without breaking it completely off? I ran around to the front of the building and tried to get in. Sure enough, the door was locked tight.

"Dad!" Julie called out. "They're about to leave!"

As much as I wanted to unravel the calamity, I'd have to let it go. I rushed over to the parking lot and held one of Joeline's hands while Julie held the other as they slid the stretcher into the back of the ambulance, her body covered in bandages.

Joeline strained to open her eyes. "Don't worry, I'm going to be fine." That about crushed me. She was a critical care nurse. She knew that might not be the case. I placed a kiss on my hand and pressed it on her foot—about the only place that wasn't bandaged or bloody, and gave her a quick wave goodbye.

The senior paramedic pulled me aside, his words clipped. "Sir, we're going west to Golden. It's a small facility, but your wife might not make it the extra twenty miles east to Banff. She's lost a lot of blood, and the bleeding hasn't stopped."

"She said no tourniquet. Was that wrong? Oh my God, I should have—"

"No, no, you did the right thing, applying pressure. If you don't know what you're doing, a tourniquet can cause severe damage."

I nodded, feeling so useless. "Can I send one of the kids with her?"

"Yes, but hurry."

I called Grace over and lifted her into the back of the ambulance. "Keep her distracted," I whispered. "Talk to her about anything. Anything at all. Just keep her mind off what's happening."

"Okay, Dad."

A young, clean-cut paramedic took hold of my arm. "I'm gonna haul ass, sir. You're free to follow me as best you can." He hopped into the cab and turned on the siren.

As the back doors shut, I heard Grace saying, "Mom, you should see the ambulance driver—he's so hot. Looks just like Tom Cruise."

11.

the sound of silence

Joeline and me on our honeymoon in 1977.
Half Dome, Yosemite Valley.

ailing the ambulance for the first six or seven miles down the
mountain was no problem. But when the driver hit the Trans-Canada Highway, he blasted off. I stayed with him until my speedometer
read ninety. This might have been exciting on a normal day, but not
then. The van was vibrating like a paint mixer, the kids clutching
anything close and stable. I had to focus on them—and not crack
under the pressure.

Should I have the kids pray for Joeline? In the passenger seat, Julie
had her knees drawn up to her chest and was biting at her fingers. I
glanced at the rest of them in the rearview mirror. Max was poking
Mollie, who wasn't returning the gesture as she typically would have.
Angela was talking quietly with one of her dolls. Except for Julie, they

seemed more subdued than worried. If we began praying for Joeline, they might get scared. So I ended up saying nothing.

But the paramedic's words kept swimming in my head.

"She's lost a lot of blood."

"The bleeding hasn't stopped."

"Your wife might not make it."

Enough! I had to stop thinking the worst. Going into a full-blown panic attack at ninety miles an hour wouldn't help us any. *Hold it together, man.*

I focused on the scenery to calm myself down. Wispy clouds stretched across the noonday sky, the valleys were deep and narrow, the road carved into the forest far enough up the slope to allow for spectacular views in all directions.

Joeline was no doubt worrying in the ambulance ahead that I was likely to drive off the edge of the cliffs attempting to keep up. That's how she operated. She was in critical condition, but was probably focusing more on our well-being than on her own.

We arrived in Golden, and I followed the signs to a hospital. When we drove into the parking lot, I wasn't sure if I was in the right place.

"Dad, there's Mom's ambulance!" Max screamed. I was never so glad to hear a screaming child.

I pulled up just past the ambulance, parked, and jumped out.

"Dad," Julie said, "you go on ahead. I'll get everybody else in."

I ran through the sliding glass doors, bracing myself for the worst. A nurse was waiting for me.

"Is she . . . ?" I couldn't get the words out.

"She's okay. Follow me. Dr. Mallard is with her."

So maybe the damage wasn't all that severe. Maybe the EMS guy was mistaken. Maybe with a few stitches Joeline would be fine.

I reached her in time to hear the doctor say, "You're stable now— you're not going to die. And you won't need a transfusion, though you've lost a lot of blood." He fumbled with his clipboard and then glanced back and forth between us. He looked about Julie's age. "I'm so sorry, but these lacerations are way too extensive for us. You'll have to be transported to Banff. They have surgeons there with much more experience. I can do a quick cleanup, but we need to get you on your way."

Joeline would have to go through the agony of the protracted trip after all. And even in Banff, would they be able to help her?

Still, I was relieved the young doctor had acknowledged he couldn't do what needed to be done, instead of proving it. He spent a few minutes cleaning out the deep wounds and administering some antibacterial shots, while apologizing repeatedly that he couldn't do more.

The staff brought Joeline a Sprite and a blanket, but to my dismay, they didn't attend to her other lacerations at all. She wasn't paying any attention to this either—not an encouraging sign. When no one was watching, I wiped off some of the dried blood from her limbs and picked out a few more tiny shards of glass.

"The doc says you're going to be fine."

"The drive to Banff is beautiful."

"I hear their hospital is one of the best in all of Canada."

Luckily my babbling fell on semiconscious ears. She smiled faintly, as if to say, "I appreciate the effort, if not the content."

The kids wanted to see Mom before we took off again. I hurried them into the ER and let them spend a couple of minutes with her. I knew Joeline was in bad shape when she could hardly raise her head to talk.

As the EMTs wheeled her down the hall toward the waiting ambulance, all of us close behind her, a woman called out, "Mr. Ohlhaut, Mr. Ohlhaut." She came running up beside me. "We need $1,800 to settle up today—in cash."

My mouth dropped. They were suddenly on the verge of having two patients in critical condition. "I don't think I have $1,800 in cash on me, but let me check." I whipped out my wallet. "Nope, $26 is all I have."

She gave me a cold stare. "Sir, we require cash payments from anyone outside of Canada. Canadian citizens are considered prepaid, but you are not. How would you like to pay?"

I didn't have time for this! But if I brushed her off, would they even take Joeline to Banff? I followed the woman to her desk and gave her my insurance card. "Here, bill these guys."

She got on the phone immediately and called them. She listened for a few moments, then frowned at me. "There's no answer."

"You must have the right number then." I gave her a weak smile. "Look, you got all the information you would have gotten had they answered the phone, and you saved yourself a lot of time."

I assured her that we were good for whatever the charges turned out to be, but most importantly, we needed to get to Banff.

So the decision to go to the closest hospital hadn't exactly paid off. But at least the bleeding was under control and Joeline's two major wounds had been cleaned, bandaged, and readied for the two-hour backtrack.

Mollie would accompany her mom in the ambulance for the next leg of the journey. The ambulance driver, for some strange reason, was intent on having Max join them for this trip. I tried to nix the idea, concerned about the consternation the little guy would likely introduce, but the driver was quite adamant about it, and Max was getting amped up about the prospect of emergency vehicle transport. He got to go along in the front seat.

Off we blasted for Banff. It was pure torture covering the same ground again. At about the halfway point, we drove past the exit for Emerald Lake, where the accident had happened. Shortly after that, I started seeing signs for the Kicking Horse Campground.

Visions of the open tent windows flashed through my mind. One side of the tent was completely exposed to the elements. Why hadn't I gone back and closed them this morning?

Most of what we had was in that tent—clothes, gear, bedding. If it rained, it would drench everything. Ruin most of it. But stopping was not an option. We had to follow the ambulance. Full speed ahead.

As we flew by the campground off-ramp, I spotted a stout black bear sitting on the hill right along the highway, eating a tree. Admittedly, it was a small tree. Or perhaps the tree wasn't that small, but the bear was that big. He had pulled the top over and was munching on it, the way a kid would eat the top off a chocolate-sprinkled ice cream cone. He was situated directly across the highway from our campsite, most likely his next stop, where he could search for s'more fixin's right through our gaping tent windows.

The drive seemed interminable. I tried to anticipate all the questions that would be coming at us over the next few hours. How best to deal with Joeline's injuries? Would we need to fly her home? How soon? Would the Banff hospital also demand cash? Where would I get thousands of dollars in cash?

I was afraid to confront the real questions. Would the surgery be successful? Would my wife be able to use her arm and hand again? Would she be able to walk?

Angela began crying. "What's wrong with Mommy? Why isn't she here?"

Grace used her own shirt to wipe away the tears. "Don't worry. Mom is fine." She put her arm around her little sister. "You know how when you fall down sometimes you get an owie? And you need a Band-Aid? Well, Mom fell down at the lake and got some owies, but we ran out of Band-Aids! So we're all going to the doctor's to get some. That way she can get all fixed up and play with us again."

This was a side of Grace I wasn't used to seeing. I was beyond grateful for her help.

The scenery appeared to change dramatically as we turned southeast toward Banff, as did the weather. It got dark, windy, and overcast, but no rain—at least where we were. Just to assure us that the rest of the world was proceeding as usual, we passed two separate campgrounds each adorned with their FULL/COMPLET signs.

We eventually passed a sign that read, "Banff—Next 3 Exits." The ambulance had traveled right at the legal maximum speed so I was able to follow it down the first exit, but I lost sight of it at the first stoplight. Thankfully, I spotted an "H" sign that directed us right to the hospital.

We parked as close as possible to the emergency room sign. Carrying Angela, I hurried inside with Julie and Grace to the information desk. The young receptionist pointed down the hall and told us that Joeline was sharing room 112 with a patient named Loren. "Sorry, but all our private rooms are occupied."

Even the hospital was FULL/COMPLET. "Do you know what happened to my two other kids?"

"An aide took them to a small patio not far from here. You'll see it on your way. Can't miss it."

Max and Mollie were sitting quietly by themselves at a picnic table overlooking a large lawn and pond. I led the rest of the kids outside and left them there, begging them with tears in my eyes to be good while I went in to be with their mom. It was pushing three o'clock, and the fuse was shortening until they combusted in hunger.

"You guys can watch the storm clouds roll in." That had to be a metaphor for something.

As I was leaving, I whispered to Julie, "Would you take care of your brother and sisters while I find Mom's room and see how she's doing?" I gave her the key to the van. "Go make some sandwiches. It's been hours since we ate anything substantial."

"Sure. Tell Mom we hope everything's okay."

I gave her a quick hug. She'd been an absolute trooper.

Jogging down the hall, I checked numbers and names on the doors and finally found Joeline's room. I nodded and smiled at her roommate, a short-haired woman about our age, and slipped past to Joeline's side by the window. She looked so worn out and tired that it tore me up inside.

I sat beside her bed and took hold of her hand. It was surprisingly warm, especially given her pale complexion. She managed a wane smile, but it lasted only a few seconds. "How . . . are the . . . kids?" she whispered, barely able to get the words out.

"They're doing fine, but they miss you." I wasn't sure what else to say to avoid worrying her, when a tall woman in a white coat strode into the room. She took off her glasses and smiled. "Good afternoon, I'm Dr. Lane. I'll be taking care of Joeline."

Hearing the confidence in her voice gave me a much-needed dose of relief.

"I just got off the phone with Dr. Mallard in Golden. He filled me in on the accident. I'd like to take a look at your injuries and then talk about how we're going to proceed." She pulled the curtain around the bed and unwrapped the bandages on Joeline's leg and arm. "Those are nasty cuts. And all this happened from falling through a window?"

"Yes," Joeline said softly. "The bathroom door . . . was jammed . . . I was trying to get out."

"I'm so sorry. And on your vacation too." Dr. Lane put her hand on Joeline's shoulder. "I need to do multilevel suturing. You'll be under full sedation and won't feel a thing. We'll get you all fixed up."

She had five other operations scheduled that evening, she said. "Your roommate is first, and I'll work you in after her."

When Dr. Lane left the room, I heard Loren say, "You're in good hands." I pulled back the curtain so we could see her.

"Dr. Lane has a great reputation," she said. "I left my four kids in Calgary and drove all this way to have her operate on an abscess in my stomach."

"I left my five kids out in the hospital yard somewhere. You can probably hear them."

She laughed. "Really, Dr. Lane is the best. I think—"

A white-gowned attendant burst into the room. "Loren, it's time to go." He started rolling her away.

"See you soon!" she called out.

Dr. Lane sounded like a godsend. Just like the couple at Emerald Lake. I sure hoped she didn't vanish before the surgery.

Joeline drifted in and out of consciousness, awaiting her turn. "I'm so sorry, Marty."

"Sorry? For what?"

"For climbing out that damn window. So stupid . . ."

"It wasn't stupid." I reminded her about the time the kid across the street took his brother's arm and broke it in half just to see if he could. "Now that was stupid." Not the best example to start this discussion, so I shut up and asked her how the ride to Banff had gone.

"Fine." She took in a long, labored breath. "Mollie kept asking the paramedics about the worst accidents they'd ever seen . . . some gruesome stories . . . knifings, car wrecks, maulings . . . I finally told her to change the subject."

"Sorry, that's my fault. I asked Mollie to get some conversation going."

"It was sorta distracting." Joeline forced a half smile.

"I should have been more specific about what kind of conversation." I glanced out the window, trying to come up with something else to say. "How's your recycled underwear holding up?"

"My underwear . . ." She closed her eyes. "It was a sign. I should have known something bad was going to happen." Then displaying more energy than I'd seen since the accident, she said, "As I was lying in that grass, the last thing I was thinking about was my dirty underwear. But it never occurred to me that I could die."

She began sobbing, almost silently.

So I'd been mistaken. She really hadn't known how serious her injuries were.

I leaned in to do something consoling, not sure what, when she opened her eyes. "Call my brother John. Ask him what he thinks of Dr. Lane's plans."

"Of course. You get some rest. I'll be back in a little while."

Off I went to find a phone.

I reached John and his wife, Terry, both of whom are medical doctors, and struggled mightily to give them a brief summary of the day's events.

I went on to describe Dr. Lane's approach to surgery.

"It all sounds reasonable to me," John said, "though I don't know much about multilevel suturing. She's going to have surgery tonight, so it won't make any difference, but I can check with a surgeon buddy tomorrow. By the way, I personally know several Canadian surgeons, and they're all top-notch."

"Dr. Lane seems wonderful, but having a second opinion would make Joel feel better."

By the time I checked on the kids, who were busy skipping stones in the pond, and then returned to the room, Loren was getting back from surgery. That meant Joeline was next. She started breathing rapidly, getting herself all worked up. I relayed John's comments and reminded her of what Loren had said, hoping that would calm her.

"It's so nice to have doctors in the family," she said.

The nurse attending to Loren came over to Joeline. "We'll be back in a little bit to get you ready. Everything's going to be just fine."

A few minutes later, the anesthetist, the surgical assistant, and the OR orderly arrived. The orderly looked down at Joeline, then over to her associates, and blurted out, "It's going to be an all-female operating room!"

"See," I said, smiling at Joeline, "they couldn't care less about your underwear. You've got a brilliant team of women working on you."

A staffer came to roll her away at about six o'clock.

"Let's do this, ladies!" she said.

"Good luck," Loren said softly, half asleep.

My insides in knots, I tried to act calm and composed as I held Joeline's hand and walked next to her down the corridor, her exhausted eyes looking up at me. They pushed her bed through a set of imposing metal doors, leaving me behind. I stood there, listening to the gurney slowly fading away.

In the solitary recesses of my mind, I could hear the sound of shattering glass—followed by silence.

12.

cry me a river

Big Blue: our home away from home for so many years.

It had grown ominously dark outside and really cold and empty inside the hospital halls. I was remembering something about Joeline
that I had let get all too dim in my mind—specifically, just how
much I loved her.

Our children were never as important to me as they were for the
next agonizing hour and a half while Joeline was in surgery. A nurse
directed us to a waiting area off the main lobby where we tried to
distract ourselves by whatever means possible. Food always did the
trick. I sent Grace to retrieve the apples from the car. She brought
back four red ones and one green one. The kids all wanted the green
apple, except for Angela, so now we had a problem.

To be as fair as possible, I put all the apples in a brown paper bag, and each of the kids got to reach in blindly and extract an apple, which they could then trade later if they could talk a sibling into agreeing. We went in alphabetical order. Angela reached in and pulled out the only green apple, throwing the whole process into disarray. She was immediately accosted by four disgruntled siblings. I had to rescue her from the barrage and begin the arduous process of convincing them that these particular red apples were actually inexplicably superior to green apples—all except for the green apple that Angela had.

And thus, we kept busy eating, watching TV, and phoning home to update the relatives. I made a few calls around Banff to check on rooms for the evening. If a comedian got as many laughs as I got making those calls, he'd be headlining in Vegas. Banff was booked solid and tight—and not just for tonight, but for the indefinite future.

At around seven-thirty, a nurse tapped me on the shoulder and whispered that Joeline was out of surgery and would be back in her room shortly. I looked into her eyes for a telltale sign of the outcome. She must have received that same look on many previous occasions. She smiled warmly. "Your wife is doing just fine."

Did she really mean that?

I leaned over to Julie. "They're bringing Mom back from surgery. Would you please stay here with everyone? I'll come get you after I check on her." I was concerned that if things weren't really "just fine," the kids didn't need to know it, or at least not yet.

By the time I reached Joeline's room, she was already there. Holy smoke, her face was so pale. Her eyelids looked like they weighed about ten pounds each—she could barely keep them open. She struggled mightily just to raise her gaze up to mine.

She slipped her left hand out from under the sheets, and I held on to it, bringing my face down to hers. I was shocked at how weak and chilly she had become. I had never seen her in such a distressed condition, barely conscious, barely alive. She mumbled something unintelligible. I lowered my ear right to her lips and she mumbled again, but I still couldn't make anything out.

"We love you, honey, and you look great."

What a lie. She looked dreadful. My heart started sinking slowly. Before it could drop all the way to the floor, Dr. Lane came in with a post-op report. "Your wife has suffered some very serious wounds, but we were able to sew her up completely, and she should have a full recovery. She's extremely lucky."

"Lucky" was definitely not the first word that came to my mind.

"Her left quadriceps was cut to the bone," Dr. Lane continued. "Severed completely in half. The glass nicked several ligaments, but caused no appreciable damage. If it had, they would have required significantly more repair work, and the recuperation time would have doubled. Had the cut gone any deeper, it would have sliced into a major artery and could have been fatal."

She paused and took a deep breath. "It's likely we wouldn't have been able to stop the bleeding."

My heart was now resting on the soles of my shoes. But the doctor kept going.

"The cut on her arm came in from the side. The glass sliced halfway through both the biceps and triceps muscles. By some miracle, it missed the nerve that controls finger movement. Had it reached that nerve, which, given the trajectory of the cut, it should have, Joeline probably would have lost much of the use of her fingers."

Maybe "lucky" *was* the right word. Or providential, or maybe just incredibly blessed.

There was a soft knock on the door, followed by Julie's voice. "Is it okay for us to come in now?"

Impeccable timing. I didn't think I could hear any more. The kids filed in so slowly and quietly I had to look closely to make sure they were ours. They gathered around the bed, shoulder to shoulder, standing at attention.

Joeline rallied just long enough to mutter, "I love you all." Then she was out again.

Grace whispered to the doctor, "How many stitches did Mom get?"

"You can't really count stitches when the wounds are this extensive," Dr. Lane said. "The sutures are done in layers and they all kind of run together."

Max stomped his foot in disappointment. "Dad, I was going to tell everyone how many stitches Mom got."

"I know, dude. We'll come up with something."

"So, like fifty?" Mollie asked.

"If I had to estimate, there are probably two hundred stitches in your mom's leg and about a hundred more in her arm. So maybe three hundred."

Now Max's face lit up. "Wow! That is so cool."

Dr. Lane smiled at him. "You know what else is pretty cool? They will dissolve all on their own. She doesn't have to come back to have them removed."

Max had no idea how serious this was—and that was a good thing. I'm not sure any of the kids really did, except for maybe Julie. The rest of them saw it as a grand adventure. Their mom went plowing through a window, shattering glass everywhere. Then they got to take turns riding in the ambulance with her, zipping around dangerous mountain curves, while the rest of the family sped behind the blaring sirens and flashing lights.

If my five kids had really understood what had just happened, that their mother narrowly escaped bleeding to death and nearly lost the use of her fingers, it wouldn't have been quite as exciting.

"Thankfully, your mom has taken really good care of herself. She's in great shape and that will help her a lot recovering. She needs a couple of days of rest and to start physical therapy as soon as she gets home. And she'll also need to avoid any undue ambulation for a while. I understand you guys are camping?"

"We are. Well, we were."

"I wouldn't recommend it, but if you have no other options, she might be okay to camp in a few days."

In a *few days*? Hell, I wouldn't be ready to camp for a few weeks, or months. Maybe never. I shot a nervous glance at Joeline. Her eyes were still closed.

"Whatever you decide to do, your wife needs to take things very slowly and carefully."

After Dr. Lane left, I sent the kids back out to the lobby once again. Pulling up the chair next to Joeline, I remembered what the doctors told me when I tore a ligament in my knee: I'd need surgery plus nine months of intense rehab. That was the moment—at age forty-two—when I realized I wasn't invincible. Now, as I sat next to Joeline, I realized she wasn't either.

I scooted my chair closer. "I can't imagine my life without you. I never thought I'd have to. Thank God you're going to be okay."

Her eyes opened just a sliver, and she smiled at me ever so faintly, murmuring something. Something sweet, I think. In this short, quiet time we had together, I talked a little more, and she slurred a little, but it was the kindest, sweetest slur I'd ever heard.

I shuddered over the horrible realization that I had been close to never hearing that sound ever again. I vowed to appreciate every slur and mumble that she blessed me with from that day on.

Joeline couldn't stay focused on anything for long. At about nine o'clock, I gave her a gentle kiss on the cheek and left her alone to get some sleep. I closed the door to her room and stared at it, reeling from everything that had happened.

What should I do now?

And oh God, where would we stay tonight? I wanted to be as close to Joeline as possible, but our campsite was our only option and it was over an hour away—how would the hospital reach us? We'd have to just hope for the best. Big Blue would give us a place to sleep, and we could pack up all our stuff and come back first thing in the morning.

I asked the staff if Grace could spend the night with her mom. In my foggy state, I interpreted their response as "no way in hell," although I'm not sure exactly what they said. I held back my initial impulsive response and instead pointed out how tiny Grace was—she could just curl up in the corner chair and wouldn't bother a soul.

The nurse conceded graciously, and the staff brought Grace blankets and pillows and offered to get her a cot. But she just curled up in the leather chair and fell asleep.

It was about ten-thirty by the time the rest of us got our stuff together and departed for the Kicking Horse Campground. Some of the emotion that would normally permeate a situation like this dissipated because of the logistical problems we had to deal with. And that was a good thing.

My plan was to pick up some fast food in Banff and then go to the campground. I cruised through the resort town only to find it as I should have expected—crammed with tourists. So I bagged the fast-food idea and told the kids to eat whatever they could find in the cooler or strewn about the van.

The winding roads on the way to Kicking Horse put the kids to sleep one by one as we drove into the dark wilderness. Even Julie, my navigator in the passenger seat, succumbed and left me alone with my thoughts. I was trying to sort through what kinds of things might befall us yet that night and what I should be prepared for the next day when Max let out a soft moan.

Uh-oh.

Seconds later, he did it again, louder.

Please, God, no more.

"Dad, I'm sick."

A shock wave rocked my body. The contaminated drinking water! Uncontrolled retching was *not* what any of us needed right now. I held my breath in silence for a moment and jammed in as many prayers as imaginable for the moaning to cease.

Five minutes went by—it felt like a year—and the little boy in the back hadn't made another peep. I kept praying softly and drove on.

About twenty minutes later, we had almost reached our campground. Up ahead, I could see a short string of red lights. The short string grew ominously longer and the red lights grew brighter until a lengthy line of traffic was backing up right in front of us.

A patrolman with a blue flashlight waved me to a stop and approached the van. My poor brain went into overload. This wasn't really happening. It wasn't midnight in the Canadian wilderness, my wife lying in the hospital recovering from a brush with death and my fatigued kids snoring in the back seats and a Canadian Mountie coming to tell me God knew what. I cracked my window.

"Sorry, sir, but you can't proceed."

I could make out a barricade beyond the blinding lights.

"The road is washed out and will be impassable for some time."

I stared at him, almost as if I didn't even see him. I tried to play back what he had just said to me. He shined his flashlight in my face, probably thinking he had a drunk on his hands. I couldn't think of anything to say to him or ask him. I simply looked at him. My attempt at mental preparation had fallen short.

I finally blurted out something like, "We have to get through. All our stuff is at the campsite and my wife is in the hospital."

Now it was his turn to stare at me. His face took on the demeanor of patient, yet fully determined authority.

"Sir, the road is closed. By which I mean the road is gone. It's part of the river now. We had torrential downpours this afternoon, and large portions of the glacier have broken loose and slid down into the river, which is now flooding way over its banks. It has washed out the highway and the railway. You can't get to your campground, if there's anything left of it. There's no telling how long the highway will be out. The only way across is by helicopter."

What the hell was he talking about? Torrential downpours? Broken glaciers? Flooding rivers? When we drove through here a few hours before, the sun was shining. Those blasted rain clouds must have parked directly above our campground, cracked open, and let loose.

Still, I had to try again. "Is there any way we can walk down to the campground or something? All our stuff is in the tent, and my wife is in the hospital." If I repeated that enough times, surely, he would make an exception.

Scowling now, he leaned down to window level. This was probably going to be his last polite response. "Sir, either your campsite has washed down the river or some disaster victim is sleeping in it. A bunch of folks are trapped on the other side of the washout, some with provisions, most without. This here's the primary railway and roadway across Canada, and we're going to work around the clock to get it opened up."

He straightened and put his hands on his hips. "Why don't you folks head back up the road to the Great Divide Lodge and get a room for the night?"

He didn't give a damn about our campsite. To be honest, if our situations were reversed, I wouldn't have given a damn about his campsite either.

I kicked myself again for not zipping up those windows. Hell, what difference would that have made? The windows were probably miles downriver by now anyway, zipped or unzipped.

Out of the depths of indecision and desperation, I was beginning to formulate my next meaningless response when another shriek pierced the night. Max was awake again and screaming. "I'm going to throw up! I'm going to throw up and die! Ahh!"

Holy Jesus! It had to be that damn water! I had visions of racing back to the hospital with Max clutching his gut and vomiting all over the back seat.

Hold on. Maybe he was having a nightmare. Maybe all the flashing lights and commotion were scaring him.

In either case, the exhausted patrolman seized the opportunity to summarily dismiss me from the highway. I put the window up, made a U-turn, sped a mile back to the lodge, and then jumped out of the van and opened the side door to contain Max.

That wasn't easy. He wasn't big for his age, but he was solid as a rock. And due to his lifelong addiction to head banging, his noggin could double as a battering ram. When he was flailing around like that, I needed to hug him real tight and tell him everything would be okay while carefully keeping my face away from his head. He almost broke my nose during a similar episode. Even just wrestling around in fun, he could inflict undue pain with his skull.

Julie had slid into the back seat and was already hugging him. She rocked him back and forth, shushing him, and he slowly calmed down. But then he must have remembered that Mom wasn't with us, and he lost it again. He writhed uncontrollably. "We have to go back and get Mom and stay with her!"

Though he was fully awake now, he wasn't very lucid, and logic wasn't taking much hold with him. It didn't take much hold when he *was* lucid, and I was coming up pretty short on logic myself. Finally, I took him from Julie and hugged him tight. Within a few minutes, his body relaxed and he looked at me strangely, as if to say, "Why are you hugging me like this?"

And just like that, his trauma had ended. I put him down on the back bench. "Everything's going to be fine, Max. Take it easy here for a minute while I run inside."

For some masochistic reason, I went into the lodge to inquire about a room. I posed my ridiculous question to the attendant, tensed in anticipation of that dreaded answer and the accompanying sarcastic snicker. He did not disappoint—on either account.

I sulked back to the van. We couldn't sleep in the tent, wherever it was, or at the lodge. That left one last option for accommodation, and we were sitting in it. And that only left one more decision—where to park it. If we were going to spend the night stuffed in the van, we might as well do it in the hospital parking lot, where, ironically, there would be fewer flashing lights and sirens then at our current location.

We began retracing our tracks to Banff. Slumber descended upon the van once again and stole my kids from me. This left me alone with my thoughts, not a place I wanted to be, but at least my thoughts had slowed to a mere trickle.

Nearing two in the morning, we pulled into a dark corner of the hospital parking lot. I woke Julie to tell her I was going in to check on Joeline.

I found Grace sound asleep in her chair, curled up like a cat. I tip-toed past Loren but the creak of the door must have roused Joeline. I was the last person she expected to see in the middle of the night, and surely she would conclude my presence could only mean that something else had gone wrong. But that wasn't information I wanted to share right then.

Instead, I whispered, "We changed our minds. We're going to stay here, just in case you needed anything. Everybody missed you, so we're going to sleep in the van out in the parking lot."

She smiled weakly and closed her eyes. I wasn't sure she heard a word I said.

I shuffled out of the hospital and toward the van in trepidation, my head hanging low. There's nothing I loathe more than trying to sleep in places that can't be slept in. If I had to choose between sleeping in a van and setting myself on fire, I don't know—it'd be a toss-up. I'm disgustingly jealous of people who can sleep in airplanes or on couches, or in vans. Especially vans. I can't do it. I don't fit comfortably anywhere except on a large bed.

This was truly an unfortunate turn of events. A little sleep would have been such a sweet reprieve.

We had rented a big van, but not quite big enough. I crammed my tall frame onto the short bench, pulling my legs up into the fetal position. Why was I even trying this? I could never sleep. What had I done in the past when I was forced to sleep in such excruciating conditions? I instantly thought of a family camping trip to the oddly named Cheesequake State Park in New Jersey when I was a kid.

It was hot and cramped, all eight of us squeezed into a small camper. Someone, most likely me, had left the flaps to our Nimrod camper open just enough to allow for a ravenous civilization of blood-thirsty mosquitoes to enter and lie in wait for my plump and juicy family to bed down for the night.

"What's going on in here!" my father hollered. Hollering was his main mode of verbal communication. I'm not sure he possessed a normal volume. "It sounds like a beehive. I'm getting eaten alive. Who left the damn flaps open?"

Knowing I would be the prime suspect—I was always the prime suspect—I retreated inside my tightly wrapped, double-insulated down sleeping bag, despite the sweltering heat of the night. This would be my sanctuary from both the mosquitoes, the majority of which had already feasted on my forehead, and my father. I just needed the mental resolve to mind-control myself to sleep.

Somehow, quite miraculously, with beads of perspiration dripping down my back and little bite mounds swelling on my cranium—and with a large chunk of paternal fear thrown in—I accomplished this task.

But lying on that bench in the van, I couldn't remember how I had made that happen.

How could I convince myself that I was comfortable?

I pretended I was sleeping in a king-size bed, surrounded by fluffy feather pillows and covered with a soft comforter. Yes, my legs were cozy, all pretzel bent, no need to straighten them out. And there's no throbbing pain shooting through my knees. This is how I would normally position my arm, hanging precipitously off the bench. If I let it dangle here for a few more minutes, hell, I wouldn't even feel it at all. And it's actually cozy having my neck bent at a forty-five-degree angle.

I managed to transform the trucks groaning past and sirens blaring in the distance into the sound of breezes rustling in the boughs of the treetops, so soothing and tranquil.

I tried this for about an hour. Then I tried something else for the next hour, and something else after that.

13.

hospitals and hospitality

Grace gracing Lake Louise, Banff National Park.

arkness turned to dimness, dimness to dawn, dawn to daylight, and drowsiness became dreariness. I think I dozed off for about thirty minutes somewhere between dim and dawn. It was during this transition from deep night to dawning day that Charles Lindbergh struggled the most to stay awake during his transatlantic flight. I was struggling to do the opposite. What's more, his trip helped him achieve worldwide fame and financial independence, while mine was ushering in disgrace and destitution.

I actually felt worse getting out of the van at seven-thirty than I did getting into it five hours before. I went into the hospital to check on Joeline.

Loren's husband was in the room tying a get-well balloon to her

IV pole. He introduced himself as Frank Walsh and gave me a firm handshake. "Loren told me what happened to you guys. If there is something we can do, please just let us know. We'd be happy to help." I thanked him, wishing there were, in fact, something he could do.

Joeline opened her eyes as I approached her bed. "How are you feeling?" I gave her a gentle peck on the cheek.

"Better, but still very tired. The nurses were in and out all night. It's impossible to sleep in a hospital."

"Keeping you awake is part of the nurse's job, you know." I smiled. "How did Grace do?"

"I'm still trying to sleep over here. Can you keep it down?"

That was my cue to go back out to the van. I pulled it around to the street just behind the hospital, a few yards from the little patio outside the back lobby area. Julie and Angela brought the cereal boxes and bowls up to the patio. This might not have been a sanctioned practice with the hospital's administration, but they probably didn't even know we were out there.

Returning to Joeline's room, I chased Grace out to join her siblings on the patio and then rolled away Joeline's breakfast tray. She hadn't touched anything—except the water.

Bracing myself, I asked, "What do you think about camping this evening, Joel? Dr. Lane thought you might be ready to leave later today." I left out the minor detail that even if she answered in the affirmative, it was probably a moot point because our tent was most likely washed up on the banks of the Kicking Horse River, miles from where we had originally pitched it.

"Camping? In a tent? I can't even get to the bathroom, just two feet away."

She didn't say this with anger—just matter of fact. Then she added, "Besides, I heard that Big Blue had drowned."

"What are you talking about?"

"The night nurse told me and Loren about the storm and the mudslide. That explains your visit in the middle of the night. I assume you slept in the van because the tent is gone."

I put my hand out to touch her but pulled back, not knowing where I could touch her without causing terrible pain. "Actually, I'm not quite sure where Big Blue is, but the rest of us are here, and we're doing okay. That's what matters. We'll figure something out. Just rest. I'll go make a few calls."

The city had set up a hotline for checking on the progress of the repair work, presuming there was any. I called it, only to find out that the extent of the damage hadn't even been determined. Likewise, the length of the outage.

We would need accommodations for at least a day or so—with Joeline hospital ridden and our belongings likely washed off the face of the earth. I asked one of the RNs if she knew where we might secure a room for a couple of days. Surprisingly, she told me that the hospital had two visitor type rooms on the first floor for folks in our predicament. Not surprisingly, both of them were FULL/COMPLET and had been for the last couple of weeks.

She led me to an office where I could use the phone. I hopped on in pursuit of that elusive inn, the one with the highly unlikely vacancy. But with every call, all I got was the usual response—laughter.

Given that hospital fees were logging in at about $1,800 a day, it seemed prudent to find out how long of a hospital stay our insurance would cover. I didn't bother calling the customer service number on the back of my card, anticipating they wouldn't answer. Instead, I went straight to the IBM benefits department. I was transferred to several agents, until one finally dared to take on the question. He sounded convincing and self-assured enough, but his actual words were vague, ambiguous—and noncommittal. Terrific. I knew less than when I started.

On to the next big issue—the potential to fly home in the next day or so.

USAir had me on this one. They would be more than happy to provide us with seven one-way tickets to Charlotte—for a hefty $4,500. This would also require a brief stopover somewhere because there were no direct flights from Calgary to Charlotte.

Optionally we could fly back to Seattle quite a bit cheaper, more in the $3,000 range, and wait for seven frequent flier seats to Charlotte to open up. Could take a day, could take a week, could take until October, plus we'd be charged a $300 reissuing fee for every ticket.

Even more overwhelmed now, I wandered back down the hall to Joeline's room. Across from the nurses' station, I bumped into Loren shuffling along using her IV pole for balance.

This was the first time I'd seen her out of her bed, and she was much shorter than I had envisioned. Her face lit up with an inviting smile. "Have you figured out what you're going to do yet?"

I shrugged and let out a long sigh. "There just aren't any good options. Come to think of it, there aren't even any bad options. Every last room in the whole of Canada appears to be booked, and flying home early isn't looking like a possibility. We can't stay at the hospital for the next week. I have no idea what we're going to do."

"I can believe it. This has been one of the warmest and busiest summers ever."

"Yes, we're learning that the hard way."

"Hey, listen, we'd really like to help you out. Frank and I were talking, and you're welcome to come stay with us. We've got plenty of room, and our kids would love it."

I straightened in disbelief. Had Loren just thrown us a lifeline? What a strange feeling—first to be struggling with such a horrible, helpless situation and then to receive such a magnanimous offer, and from folks who hardly even knew us, except that our wives had randomly been placed in the same hospital room.

My normal reaction would have been to jump at an invitation like this, but it simply wasn't practical. As Loren told me about her son and three daughters, I quickly did the math: together, there would be nine kids, five of them under the age of ten—along with two incapacitated mothers and two hapless dads. Well, one hapless dad invading another dad's home. They'd probably end up bouncing us out after a few hours of chaos.

"Thank you, Loren, but that's just too much . . . inconvenience, disturbance, pandemonium, especially with everything you've got going on." My usual impeccable articulation had deserted me. "This is so kind of you, but we'll figure something out." This was more of a wish than a fact.

Seeing her face fall in disappointment, I quickly added, "But can we keep that option open as a backup plan?" I didn't want to appear ungrateful.

Loren reiterated that they really would like us to come. "If my family was out of the country and injured and stranded, I'd like to think that someone would help take care of us. I'm sure you would do the same if the situation were reversed, wouldn't you?"

My mind went blank. Joeline certainly would—and I certainly would, right after Joeline told me to. I nodded.

"Besides, your kids have been so well behaved, it really wouldn't be a problem."

I had to stop myself from laughing at that one. She hadn't seen their true colors yet.

"I'm going home today, but please think about it," she said. "I'll leave you my number and you can call anytime to let us know what you decide."

As Loren continued on down the hallway, I leaned against the wall, feeling uneasy about accepting accommodations from someone I didn't know very well—for their sake *and* ours. Couzy's brother immediately came to mind.

Pinky had seemed harmless enough the first few days we stayed with him in LA. But we should have known better.

One afternoon he took Walt and me into his garage to show us his hogs—his Harley-Davidson motorcycles. Two beautiful Great American Freedom Machines, surrounded by thousands of bike parts scattered everywhere.

As the most ardent motorcyclist of our wayward group, I voiced the astute observation, "There must be a fortune in parts lying around here."

"Yes! An absolute fortune," Pinky said. "But there's a bit of a dispute about ownership."

He told us that his former brethren—the local Hells Angels gang—believed this contraband belonged to them. We gave out a faint chuckle, wrestling with the implications of this outrageous claim and curious about its veracity.

Sensing our disbelief, Pinky puffed up. "Follow me, boys."

He led us up into the attic and displayed his mounted fully automatic, fully loaded machine gun. We'd never seen one before except in the movies.

Pinky patted it, almost lovingly. "This beauty is designed to fire at the rate of 250 rounds a minute. That should slow 'em down."

We stood there stupefied, our jaws hanging open.

"I'm never quite sure if or when they're coming to retrieve their hardware. But I'm ready when they do."

I wasn't worried that Loren was dealing in stolen motorcycle parts or packing heat up in her attic. After all, they rode horses around here, not hogs. But I still couldn't accept her offer.

Joeline agreed. "It's so kind of them, but we could never impose like that." She turned her head away from me as a tear slid down her cheek.

"What's wrong?"

"I ruined our vacation. We were looking forward to this for so long. We didn't come all the way to the Canadian Rockies to stay with strangers or sit around a hospital." She was sobbing now.

"It was an accident, Joel. And if you want, we can fly you home. Maybe you and Julie can fly back together. She doesn't like camping anyway, so you'd be doing her a favor." I smiled.

She took a deep breath. "No, I'm not leaving you guys. I'll stick it out here. I never should have climbed out that stupid window."

"I would have done the same thing."

"That's why I did it! I didn't want to make us late for the canoe ride, and I thought, well, Marty would just climb out the window. You would have made it through just fine, but I practically got myself killed."

"If you couldn't make it out, I never would have either."

Joeline laughed a little, wiping her face with a Kleenex.

"We don't have to decide anything right now, honey. It will all work out."

Joeline needed to rest. She and the nurses agreed it would be best if we vacated the premises for a few hours. A fine idea, but where to vacate to? Regardless, we needed to leave her alone for a few hours and then come back and assess her condition,

I packed up all five kids, and we drove most of the way to the Kicking Horse Campground before detouring off to the magnificent Lake Louise. Snow-covered rocky mountain peaks engulfed the surroundings, the tops of the tall pines stretched into the sky while their trunks cradled a turquoise lake that reflected the sky as precisely as a mirror. It could have been the most beautiful place on earth—if mankind hadn't discovered it and commercialized it. The easterly view offers a freakish combination of Disneyland, Ringling Brothers, and the Cowtown Rodeo.

The Fairmont Chateau standing on the grounds is both grand and gross at the same time. An overwhelming behemoth of a structure, carved into the most gorgeous countryside, it's a stark intrusion on the natural terrain—a silk carnation among flourishing wildflowers.

We made our way down to a rustic stone wall set in along the eastern shore, the perfect place to sit and enjoy our lunch and the superb view out to the mountains, away from the circus behind us.

To get even farther away from the chateau, we hiked up into the hills, in the general direction of the famed Lake Agnes Tea House,

constructed by the Canadian Pacific Railway back in 1901. We had
to stop every five steps to toss stones into the lake, so we didn't get
far. The Canadian Rockies have a lot of rocks—enough to keep five
children sufficiently detained from attempting the Tea House trek.

It was also a requirement that since we were indefinitely removed
from our clothing supplies, someone would fall into the lake. Angela
stepped up to the challenge, but it was only a partial submersion and
somehow related to stone tossing. Wringing out her clothes, I decided
it was time to move on to dryer pastures.

As I drove the van down the park exit, the condition of our campsite began preying on me. I tried to push those concerns into one
of the many empty recesses of my mind, but to no avail. Spotting a
pay phone at the park entrance, I pulled over and called the hotline.

According to the recorded message, they hadn't made any progress. This only increased my obsession with our gear. Was it still
there? Was it floating down the river? Had it been dispersed among
the stranded campers? We were near the campground already and
could easily invest another twenty minutes to uncover the fate of
our belongings.

Off we went to Kicking Horse. All too quickly, we came upon a
menacing roadblock, which I very quickly drove around. We then
quickly came upon another one, which unfortunately was guarded
by a patrolman who seemed intent on stopping us.

I lowered my window. "Any chance we can get into the campground? We'd really like to know what happened to the tent we
pitched in there the other night."

"Don't know. You're welcome to drive on ahead and get behind
those other cars. A patrol vehicle will be coming to escort everyone
through. We're not sure how long the temporary dams are going to
hold, though. The highway might flood again."

Temporary dams? That only made me more determined to learn
the state of our belongings. And maybe rescue them before their state
downgraded radically. We drove forward and joined the cars lined
up for the escort.

I couldn't have asked for a more fantastic view to distract me from my anxiety. We were sitting right next to the bottom of a high snowcapped-mountain divide, its jagged chutes running parallel all along the face. A pristine lake separated us from the mountain base and served as the mountain's identical twin.

Tired of waiting, the kids bolted out of the van before I could stop them and amused themselves by trying to balance along the guardrails. Watching them struggle helped raise my gloomy spirits, to the point where I hopped out to show them how it was done.

It took me three or four attempts before I could even get up on the rail and then three or four seconds before I fell off—amid howls of laughter. I was only spared further embarrassment by the sound of engines starting up, indicating that the line was about to move forward.

In just a half hour, the sky had grown dark and foreboding. The winds at the mountain peaks sent trails of snow hundreds of feet out into the brownish green skies. It was unsettling how fast the overall mood of the surroundings had changed.

The escort started down the highway, the line looking interminable. Fifty cars must have been in front of us as we descended down into the valley. About a mile to the Kicking Horse exit, we came across a couple of bulldozers working along the hillside. Two rangers stood next to the road. I pulled over, leaned out the window, and asked about the campground.

"Sorry, sir, the entrance is still washed out."

"Is there another way in? We set up a campsite two days ago, and we're trying to find out if anything's left of it."

One of the rangers came over to us and pointed to a section of flattened mud up ahead. "They just bulldozed that path through the woods down to the campground for park vehicles. It's slippery and steep in places. I guess you can give it a try. Getting down should be fairly easy, but driving back up might be a different story." He looked at the storm clouds rumbling overhead. "Unless you've got four-wheel drive on this thing." He rapped on the hood.

I didn't. Obviously. But I really needed to know if our stuff had survived. If Big Blue had in fact drowned, we were going to have a very serious problem. So I drove ahead to the mud path.

Taking in an enormous breath, I cranked my eyes so wide open I could feel a breeze deep in their sockets, and down we went. We had gone about a hundred yards, or 93.3 meters, as I had come to learn in this metric land, when the path swerved gradually to the left. I turned the wheel gently in that direction, but the van proceeded gently straight.

Hold on! That wasn't supposed to happen. I wiggled the wheel back and forth, frantically trying to regain traction, and then tapped the breaks. The back wheels began sliding to the right as the van picked up some speed. I couldn't make out what lay directly in front of us, but I sure as hell didn't want to slide into it.

This was much worse than the ranger said—or at least what I thought he said.

Grace and Max started getting juiced about the ride, not realizing that their short lives might soon be cut even shorter. I held down the brakes, hoping the back wheels would lock and maybe even drift to the left. Crazy enough, that was exactly what happened. When I released the brakes, the van slid ahead, now roughly following the contour of the road.

The hill was in fact very steep and slippery—the ranger was spot on about that. As we continued on, when I let off the brakes, we became quick runaways, and when I rode the brakes, the van kept slipping and sliding in all directions.

Right about now, I started to wonder how much we really needed to know if Big Blue had survived. Maybe we could sleep in the van for eight more nights. I would be certifiable, but that would keep me from wiping out my family on this luge run—or from suffering the angst of having to find more empty campsites.

It was too late, though. Busting a U-turn wasn't going to happen without direct intervention from God, and I had already over-taxed that line of support. The path eventually leveled out across a clearing, shot up a small lip, and deposited us somewhere in the campground.

I let out a sigh of relief. Thank you, Lord!

As I rounded a bend, afraid of what we'd find, or not find, I caught a glimpse of old Big Blue, the only tent still standing, now only fifty feet from the river. Sure enough, the easterly windows, zipped up tight, had resisted the fury of the storm. Just then, a beam from the setting sun broke through the swirling gray clouds and shone on our campsite for a few glorious seconds.

I parked the van, jumped out, and rushed over to inspect the tent. My jaw dropped. Everything inside was bone dry. How could it rain hard enough to melt a glacier, trigger a mudslide, and flood a river, but not wash our tent away, or at least completely drench it?

As the kids rummaged through their things in disbelief, the heavens opened. Sheets of rain poured down, accompanied by crushing thunder and wild bolts of lightning, and we frantically zipped up the windows.

We might as well stay put and enjoy the rainstorm. Be good sleeping weather. Not that I was going to require any special weather conditions to sleep well.

"Guys, we're staying here tonight," I said. Finally, something had worked out for a change.

"Yay!" the kids shouted.

"I love sleeping in thunderstorms."

"It feels good with the wind blowing."

"And the lightning is so cool."

I picked up Joeline's empty sleeping bag. "But we have a problem. We've got to call Mom and let her know we're planning to stay here tonight."

How was I going to do that? Once again, I got the feeling that although it didn't seem like a big deal, it was probably going to turn into one.

We waited for a small break in the rain and then drove to the ranger booth where we'd checked in two days earlier in far better straits. What a surprise to find someone on duty.

"Thank God you're here. Can we please use your phone?"

"Sorry, sir, but all we have is radio, and it can't be used for anything except emergencies."

"This is an emergency."

"You can try the Cathedral Mountain Lodge, right across the road there. They probably have a phone you could use."

I pulled into the parking lot, popped inside, and asked the woman at the desk if I could use their phone. "My wife's in the hospital and—"

She cut me off. "I'd absolutely let you use our phone if it were working. But I'm afraid the storm knocked it out. I heard the Great Divide Lodge up the road has power. You could give that a try."

A wave of despair washed over me. Now I had a real dilemma. A trip to the Great Divide Lodge would require driving up the mud path. Going down that sloppy morass had been a questionable undertaking. Attempting an accent might land us at the undertaker. And would the path hold out in all this rain for us to make it back down again? Maybe we should pack everything, drive to Banff, and sleep in the van another night?

Two bad options. Both required going up the mud run, and since everyone was already in the van, I went for it. At the bottom of the path, I gunned it. For some inexplicable reason, the ride up wasn't nearly as life threating as the ride down.

The line of cars on the highway was completely gone, no escort in sight. We arrived at the lodge in under five minutes, and I was inside in under five seconds, my tattered MCI card in hand, explaining my plight to the desk clerk.

"You don't need that card, sir. You can use one of the phones down the hall."

I eventually reached the nurse's station and asked to be patched through to Joeline.

"She was sleeping the last time I checked, but let me wake her up for you. Hang on."

Before I could get out "No! Let her sleep!" I heard Joeline's exhausted voice. Clearly, she was heavily sedated and had not, in fact, been pondering our whereabouts.

I began relaying the good news about our campsite when something scampered across my foot. I looked down to see a gray squirrel barreling toward the end of the hall, followed by a large black Lab at full tilt, barking and yelping madly. The dog treed the squirrel in the curtains behind me.

In the crushing racket, all I could do was bellow into the phone, "Joel, don't hang up! We've got a wildlife situation here." The squirrel came flying back away from the curtains, across my feet, and out the open front door, the dog right on his bushy tail.

Bright orange and red triangles started floating across my vision—a full-blown migraine wasn't far away. Taking a deep breath, I said to Joeline, "Honey, we need to accept the Walshes' offer. If you feel up to it, can you please call them in the morning? And I'm sorry for waking you."

I hung up and saw that my five kids had followed me inside and were fidgeting and knocking things over, soon to transition from hunger to hysteria. I needed to rectify this quickly. Spotting a lodge attendant, I asked her if they could they spare a few crumbs to help us stave off the demons. Cooking over a campfire in the rain had the same appeal as lying prostrate on an ant hill.

"I'm sorry, sir," I heard for about the tenth time that day. "The kitchen closed about fifteen minutes ago." At least she seemed genuinely sorry.

"By any chance do you think there might be some leftovers? We'd take scraps at this point."

She took pity on me and went off to talk with the kitchen staff, returning almost immediately. "The cooks are putting together a couple of sandwiches. Ham and cheese okay?"

"That's way more than okay. Thank you!"

"Be ready in a jiffy."

She darted off. And indeed, she returned in an absolute "jiffy." I graciously accepted the food, and they graciously rejected my attempt to pay for it. So I tipped them with the few remaining Canadian bills in my wallet, and we scurried to the van.

I pulled off the highway at our favorite mud run with immeasurable trepidation. No rangers were in sight, and it was still drizzling. I thought I caught a glimpse of the taillights of some gutsy vehicle exiting the luge below.

With no more consideration than that, I lurched the van forward. I don't know what I did differently going down the path this time, but I held the wheel steady, never exceeding one mile (1.3 kilometers) an hour, and apparently that did the trick. We reentered the campground unceremoniously and began to wind our way back to our site.

Turning the corner, I was startled to discover an untold number of people lying on the ground in sleeping bags in the campsite across the road. Many of them spilled into ours. I stopped the van and stared at them. They appeared generally comatose as they stared back.

They must have been some of the poor souls the patrolman mentioned, left stranded by the flood. The standoff ended peacefully when the folks in our site surrendered ground and reluctantly moved. We piled out and reoccupied our territory.

The evening storm had finally subsided, leaving the night damp and chilly. We huddled around the dripping picnic table and gobbled down our gourmet dinner.

I ushered the kids into the tent, telling them I'd be in shortly.

Just beyond our campsite, I sat on a wet log. One week ago, I was in Charlotte with my beautiful wife, snuggled in our warm, dry bed, so excited for this blowout vacation. How quickly things could change.

What was it the priest had said? "You will be tested by unexpected circumstances and hardships. Deal with them humbly, knowing they're a part of God's plan, and this will help you appreciate all the blessings in your life."

Not sure how humble I'd been through everything, but I was certainly getting a crash course on what really mattered.

Joeline would make a full recovery. It might take months, but there'd be no permanent damage. My shoulders drooped and my migraine faded as my body started to relax for the first time since I saw her covered in blood.

Our family was going to be okay.

I joined everyone in the tent as quietly as I could, about as quiet as a mariachi band. Eventually, I began to drift off, recalling how our friend James Hector had nearly died here decades earlier. Joeline had nearly died too. But they both survived.

Tomorrow I would salvage what was left of our last great camping adventure—although I had no idea how.

14.

lost and found

The Walsh family.

I woke to the sounds of Kicking Horse River, still in awe that Big Blue and all our possessions had survived. Buoyed by that act of mercy and a good night's sleep, I was motivated to get back in the proverbial saddle. We'd spend the morning exploring as we slowly made our way to Banff. Joeline needed more time to rest before hopefully being released later in the day.

For once we could leisurely load the van, without me being a taskmaster. Last to go in was our stash of firewood. Piled next to the firepit, it had soaked up every drop of rain in the area, and the cardboard boxes had disintegrated into mush. Hauling wet logs around would be extremely messy. But we'd probably end up camping again at some point, most likely in the States, and unlike the Canadians, who had so graciously provided for our pyrotechnical needs, the Americans did *not* offer complimentary wood. Sighing, I grabbed an armload of buggy, damp logs and tossed them into the back of the van.

Thankfully, the crews had worked all night on the main campground road and we could exit the area without revisiting the slick mud path.

Our first stop on the way to Banff was the Canadian Pacific Railway's dueling Spiral Tunnels. If you're lucky, you can watch a train snake its way down the mountain, crossing beneath itself twice, forming a rough figure eight. Unfortunately, it's hard to grasp this feat of engineering without a train to demonstrate how it works. Of the twenty-five to thirty trains that traverse those tracks daily, we saw exactly none of them.

So we continued on and reached the roadblock from the night before. Several hundred cars queued up for what a ranger had told us was about a six-hour wait. People had abandoned their vehicles and were sitting out in lounge chairs, having picnics, playing catch, or just enjoying the scenery. Some were even trying to balance on the guardrails. Good thing we were going in the opposite direction. I continued east toward Moraine Lake, our second detour on the way to the hospital.

We had the whole place to ourselves. I can't understand why Moraine Lake isn't as popular as Lake Louise. It is every bit as beautiful, so stunning, in fact, that it's featured on the 1969 and 1979 Canadian twenty-dollar bill.

Always eager to infuse a little education into our outings, I asked the kids if they could guess the names of the ten jagged mountain peaks flanking the far end the lake. "It's very simple," I said.

Grace rolled her eyes. "I have no idea," she said, though now she was curious. Julie stared at the peaks in quiet contemplation.

"Give me a clue," Mollie said. She usually enjoyed these informative interludes.

"What is the Count from *Sesame Street* famous for?"

That hint didn't help Mollie or Grace. Max was too busy throwing stones into the lake. Angela was oblivious to the lesson. "The Count?" Julie repeated. "One, two, three, ah-ah-ah?" She did her best impression of the Count's laugh. I don't think this was an actual guess as much as it was just an imitation. But it was close enough.

"Exactly!" I said. "Their names are One, Two, Three, Four, Five, Six, Seven, Eight, Nine, and Ten."

"Dad, no offense, but that doesn't sound right," Grace said.

"Yep, it's true. Samuel Allen was one of the first people to explore this area and that's what he named the mountains. But you're right, Grace, there's a catch. He named them in the Nakoda Indian language. So that peak to the right is One, Neptuak. And that last one over there is Ten, Wenkchemna." I swept my hand across the horizon.

"To confuse you even more, somewhere along the way, they renamed most of the peaks after famous people. Peak Six is now Mount Allen."

By this point, everyone except Julie had walked off and joined Max in throwing rocks in the water.

The educational portion of the day now complete, I let the kids play on a huge pile of rocks and boulders maybe twenty feet high. They ascended the hill in tumultuous fashion, then proceeded to push each other off. It was the perfect playground—tall enough to be challenging, steep enough to be scary, and rocky enough to be a little dangerous. Good fun—minimal suffering.

We had managed to burn up most of the afternoon, but we had one more stop to make. Joeline needed clean clothes—which meant new clothes—and I needed to get them. We drove back to Banff, parked at the hospital, and made our way on foot to the bustling shopping district around the corner.

Shopping for clothes, particularly for someone else, is one of my favorite pastimes. It ranks right up there with removing fishhooks from my backside. I was especially looking forward to doing it with my five hyperactive children.

When shopping, I use the "first in, last out" approach. I go into the first store I see and buy the first thing that resembles what I'm looking for, and then this store becomes the last one I step out of. Aware that this approach might not yield the best results, I asked Julie to take charge.

Given Joeline's inability to use crucial body parts, namely her arm and leg, Julie had to choose attire that would lend itself to her disabilities while being at least somewhat fashionable. This wasn't an easy task, but we bought two sundresses that would suffice—along with plenty of underwear.

When we arrived at the hospital, Joeline was sitting up in bed and some of the color had returned to her face. She nodded toward a prescription on the bedside tray and asked me to get it filled.

This pleased me, seeing how we had just walked directly past the drugstore on our way back to the hospital. But Joeline would definitely need some drugs later on to manage the pain. I might take a few myself. Before we took off again, she told me that she had called Loren. "She said that we're more than welcome to stay with them as long as we need."

Embarrassed for not handling the situation myself, I was also beyond relieved that we had a place to stay for the immediate future. My neck and shoulders loosened ever so slightly more. I made a resolution to be more like the Walshes in the future.

"And go to the grocery store while you're out. I'm not about to show up at their house without a crumb of food."

The kids and I walked to the drugstore first. Like Americans, the Canadians have not devised a way of reducing the wait time. Even if you're the only person in the store, you must wait some predetermined amount of time before the pharmacist will look down and acknowledge your presence, take your prescription, peck away at a computer screen, rummage through a mountain of pills, and then package up a few for you. While we waited, I loaded up on Band-Aids and gauze, figuring they might come in handy.

Next, we crossed the road and ventured into the grocery store. Shopping for groceries is just a notch above shopping for clothes.

But I could be less decisive in the grocery store, as my children ran up and down the aisles throwing cookies and doughnuts and Fritos into the cart, taking full advantage of the situation, knowing I was too tired to care and Mom wasn't there to stop them. Julie attempted to control the hungry mob, occasionally putting things back on the shelves but with little success.

Once outside the grocery store, a bag in each hand, I was determined to take a shortcut back to the hospital. Not that I had any idea where one was, but we came from the right, so my keen sense of direction set us off to the left. Twenty minutes later, and still no hospital in sight, it occurred to me that it had taken us only five minutes to walk from the hospital to the drugstore, and then another five minutes to get to the grocery store. At this point, my shortcut had about doubled our return time, and while I would never admit it, I was totally lost.

Alas, my children had reached the age when they could tell I had goofed up. I used to be able to confuse and distract them, but now they were staring at me, ready to follow, despite knowing that I had no idea where we were going. I glanced desperately around every corner we came to, only to have my hopes dashed by the unfamiliar terrain. I wasn't even sure I could get us back to the grocery store at that point.

Nevertheless, I thrust out my chest, stood tall, and strode ahead, trying to convince the kids I knew where we were going. We wandered and roamed, and finally, I spied the hospital—across a divided, four-lane road. How was that possible? How did we end up on the other side of a road we never crossed? For a moment I debated dashing across, but I didn't want any of the little ones to end up as a hood ornament.

Instead, we walked several more blocks in the opposite direction to safely use a designated crosswalk and then continue back down on the other side of the street. Only about three times longer than shooting across, but significantly safer.

Feeling great solace that we had all made it back to the hospital, I walked into Joeline's room with a bounce in my step.

"Martin, where have you been? I've been worried to death!"

"Uh, yes, well, we got lost." I surveyed my tired brood. "I got us lost. It's tricky out there."

"I'm just glad you're back. The nurse came in a minute ago and said they're going to discharge me. I need you to help me get ready to go."

"Why don't we start by getting these new clothes on you?" I pulled the two dresses from the bag. "Julie and Grace, will you help your mom?"

I drew Joeline's curtain around the three of them, and asked Mollie to gather up the few things Mom had lying about.

I poked my head around the curtain and saw for the first time just how bandaged up Joeline was. A pit formed in my stomach. Her right arm, from elbow to shoulder, and her left leg, from knee to hip, were wrapped with gauze and tape to about twice their normal circumference. She was half mummy, half mommy. And a myriad little Band-Aids crisscrossed her body, covering all the smaller glass cuts.

Thank God the nurse told Joeline not to change the bandages until we were back in Charlotte. I would never have gotten her rewrapped.

The nurse also said that Joeline would get instructions on how to get around with her many infirmities. But that never happened. A cane had appeared in the corner of the room, and we assumed it was for her.

We kept thinking someone would arrive with a wheelchair—but that didn't happen either. I finally told Grace and Max to go find one.

In seconds, they came flying back into the room laughing hysterically, Max pushing Grace in a wheelchair as she held on for dear life. I looked from the chair to Joeline and back again. How would we transfer her from the bed?

"Get a bedsheet," Joeline told Mollie. "I have an idea."

Mollie immediately snatched the sheet off the bed.

"Marty, you come here and help me stand up. Mollie, wrap the sheet around me. Now, very slowly, as you hold on to the sheet, lower me down into the chair."

Success! We were ready to roll.

As we approached the exit doors, we finally received some assistance. The receptionist wanted to assist me in paying them $5,800 in cash before departing.

I looked over the one-page invoice she had handed to me. How did $1,800 a day times two days come to $5,800? There weren't *that* many Band-Aids. But I'd learned that a hospital can pretty much charge you whatever they feel like, and there's nothing you can do except pay up.

Since I had gained a little experience in this process, I extended my insurance card. The seven of us gathered around, watching her dial the number on the back of the card. We all stood by quietly and waited and waited. Finally, she handed the card back to me. "There's no answer."

"Then you've dialed the right number." I called over my shoulder as I wheeled Joeline out through the sliding glass doors.

15.

heaven on earth

Me riding Junior in the Mule Mountains, Bisbee, Arizona, 1970.

We came to a grinding halt at the van. How the heck would we get Joeline inside? All the kids lined up next to her and looked at me for direction. This was going to take some serious planning.

The first step: getting Joeline out of the chair. That actually wasn't too bad. With the sheet in place, we simply hoisted her up into a standing position.

But getting her through the narrow van door was a different story. We somehow twisted and contorted her through the door, guiding her up and back without touching any of the many places that hurt, landing her on the passenger seat.

The rest of the family piled into the van, and I sped off in the direction of Calgary hoping to avoid Friday afternoon traffic. My stomach churned at what lay ahead. The Walshes had been extremely kind and generous in the hospital. But we would soon overrun their home—would we overrun their generosity?

So far, our trip had been like riding a seesaw—highs and lows, ups and downs. Was it time to go up?

To contribute to the likelihood of an ascent, I needed to get the kids' buy-in. "Listen up, everyone. We all have to be on our very best behavior while we're staying with the Walshes. I can count on each of you to pitch in and help, right?"

"Sure, Dad. No problem."

They didn't sound overly sincere. A brief reference to the consequences of deviation might be appropriate. "Everybody behaves, nobody gets hurt. Okay?"

A silence fell over the van.

And thus, we established an inviolate pact—a pact that good behavior would be rewarded with longevity, but any deviation from this behavior might result in an untimely demise.

It was more of a unilateral pact.

About an hour out of Banff, we got off the Trans-Canada Highway. Joeline struggled to decipher the directions she had scribbled down with her left hand as the kids refrained from making any jokes about being lost. We drove a short distance through the beautiful countryside, with very limited signage, and took a road we hoped would lead to their home.

We were supposed to count three houses on the right and then turn into their long driveway. Simple enough, until out of the blue we came upon a large tepee that appeared to be inhabited. Did it count as one of the three houses? Would we pull up the Walshes' driveway, only to end up at an enormous tepee, Frank standing in front waving "hello" and wearing a massive feather headdress?

Then I spotted their mailbox and their house up on the hill to the right: a beautiful mansion overlooking the city of Calgary, a beacon in the darkness.

We were going up on the seesaw.

All four Walsh children ran around the expansive front yard guarded protectively by the family dog, as horses grazed peacefully off in the distance. Our arrival would likely put an end to all this serenity.

It took a couple of minutes to wind along their driveway and eventually pull up to the house. Frank emerged promptly to greet us. Before I could utter a word of caution, our kids had emptied out of the van and joined the others in running through the sprinkler in the yard, laughing and screaming.

Joeline's condition had declined steadily through our hour-long drive, and she was now feeling weak and nauseated. We needed to get her out of the van immediately. But we couldn't remember exactly how we got her in, and reversing a process that we couldn't recall wasn't going to be easy. Frank graciously joined in to help extricate Joeline from the van. Though a broad, strapping fellow—we would later find out he was a hockey player—he was gentle and meticulous in maneuvering around her bad leg, but then inadvertently grabbed her bad arm around the stitches.

Joeline would never intentionally hurt someone's feelings, especially when that someone was trying to help her. But the bolt of pain made her cry out, "Oh, God!"

Frank jumped back. "Geez, I'm so sorry!"

"It's okay," I said. "Having both a bad leg *and* a bad arm makes it really tricky."

I felt terrible for Frank, and for Joeline. He pulled back and left this final transportation issue to us.

Once I managed to get Joeline out of the van and on firm ground holding onto her cane, she said softly, "Can we just stop here a minute? My head is spinning."

"Take as long as you need, honey. There's no hurry."

We stood for a few moments in the driveway, Joeline wavering back and forth between me and Julie, who had refrained from the chaos. When we got to the front porch, I saw trouble: just a single step, but for Joeline, it might as well have been Mount Everest—and it was slippery, thanks to our children hosing it down with the sprinkler moments before.

She pleaded for another break. Julie brought a patio chair over, and we helped her ease into it. We considered carrying the chair with her in it, but one little slip could be disastrous.

As we waited, I caught sight of Loren, watching all this through a second-story window, presumably where she was recuperating from her own surgery. Oh boy! She had to be wondering what she'd gotten herself into.

Joeline said she was ready. We helped her up from the chair and over to the step. Applying the "good foot goes to heaven, and the bad foot goes to hell" mantra, she stepped up with her sound leg. And with some locomotive assistance from behind, she made it over the final hurdle and through the front door, slumping down onto the closest couch.

Frank handed her a glass of cold lemonade. She took one sip, passed it on to me, and leaned her head back. I would have welcomed a sip of Jack Daniels myself. As I sat next to Joeline, hoping to console her, I heard piercing screams. Oh right, we had brought five kids with us, and it sounded like at least a couple of them were now in direct violation of our pact.

I slid out the back door and found all the kids jumping wildly around on the Walshes' trampoline. They really weren't misbehaving, but I needed to set the bar high.

"This is your only warning! Keep the ruckus down, or I'll be forced to execute the pact—and you." Max didn't know what "execute" meant, but one of his older sisters would explain it to him.

Frank was getting dinner sorted, and I jumped in as his sous-chef. We put together a fine offering of burgers, hot dogs, chips, beans, and baked potatoes. Neither of us dawdled, knowing that the kids were approaching their cracking point. My kids showed no warning sign—one minute they would be playing, and the next, they would become insufferably obnoxious.

Loren joined us, doing well with her own recovery, and we all sat around their large dining room table. I took a seat where I could keep an eye on Joeline in the family room. Just as everyone was lifting forks to mouths, she started groaning, and then leaned over and threw up. Frank quickly opened all the doors and windows, and I ran back and forth, emptying barf buckets and serving burgers and beans.

Once the crisis passed and everyone was fed, Joeline asked me to help her downstairs to the bedroom where she would be sleeping. After considerable deliberation, she and I played a bit of piggyback, her good arm wrapped around my neck and me bent over at a forty-five-degree angle. We summoned the little guys and had them squeeze alongside, helping Joeline stay balanced on my back, Frank judiciously observing from a few feet away.

We gave those handrails a firm workout, slowly making our descent, and then trundled into one of the bedrooms where Frank had made up a bed. I helped Joeline slide under the covers. She was asleep before I finished lifting her bandaged leg in beside her.

The Walshes' nanny was out of town for the weekend, so the entire bottom floor of their home was available to us. We had ample space for all of us and our belongings. Frank told me they had cleared their calendar for the weekend, setting aside recovery time for Loren. He would have to go back to work on Monday, but we could stay as long as necessary.

How could we ever repay such generosity?

I sat alone with Joeline for a few minutes, but she was zonked. When the doorbell rang and I heard unfamiliar voices, I gave her a quick kiss on the cheek, evoking zero response, and then hustled up the stairs.

Neighbors Allin and Alice had stopped over and offered to take the older girls for a short horseback ride. I've never seen Grace move so fast. If she could have pulled it off, she would have abandoned our family completely and begged Allin and Alice to adopt her. She, along with Julie and Mollie, went riding off into the sunset, before the doors could swing shut.

Watching them leave, I wished I could have joined them. I hadn't spent a full day in the saddle since my twentieth birthday, when I had the opportunity to spend two weeks visiting my uncle Leroy, out in Bisbee, Arizona, right on the Mexican border. He used to ride Brahman bulls in rodeo shows all over the West. Straddling these huge, strong animals for a living left him with a distinct wishbone stance.

Uncle Leroy and Aunt Marianne lived on a few hundred acres amid the endless expanse of prickly pear cactus, century plants, and rattlesnakes that fill the desert between Bisbee and Tombstone. Many afternoons I rode between the two towns once frequented by Wyatt Earp, Doc Holliday, and the Clanton gang. A cowboy could ride for hours, unobserved and undisturbed, in any direction, his only company being the shadows of the clouds blowing across the wasteland and the spirit of Geronimo.

Uncle Leroy would saddle up his old mare Junior for me and attach a .22 rifle to the saddle in case I needed it. I had never fired a rifle before, so one day I figured I should practice. But the desert doesn't offer much in the way of targets. There were plenty of cacti to abuse, though they were so chewed up to begin with that it would be impossible to determine if you'd made contact with one or not.

But plenty of rocks were lying around, so I got the bright idea of lining up several along a low ridge and trying to shoot them off. I fired away for a while, delighted by being so far away from anybody and anything that I couldn't possibly cause any trouble. Occasionally a rock would spin or twist as I fired away. A couple even slid off the back. But mainly dust just flew up behind the rocks as my bullets sped harmlessly into the barren solitude.

I took aim at one of the bigger rocks, hoping to drill it on the first shot. Blam! I nailed it, or one of its neighbors, dead center. As the rock spun off the ridge, something whistled right past my head.

Was that my bullet? Holy shit!

I didn't need to practice anymore. And I sure as hell didn't need to tell anyone how I discovered that rocks didn't make for good targets.

As darkness fell, the girls returned to the house from their ride, raving about the fun they'd had and the beautiful horses. Soon after, Frank started a small bonfire in the firepit so the kids could roast marshmallows. I didn't have the heart to tell him that our kids had been roasting marshmallows every night for the past week.

I was only half paying attention anyway, alternately worrying about Joeline and being entranced by the view from their backyard. An electrical storm threw branches of lightning sporadically across the sky, illuminating the Rockies to the west. To the east, a million tiny lights glowed in the city of Calgary. All around me, the wind swooped down and tangoed with the fire's embers, lifting them up into the night sky.

16.

the pieman cometh

The pieman Allin and his wife, Alice, circa 2005.

Under normal circumstances, sleeping on a foldout sofa bed rates just a notch above sleeping on a van bench. But it was pure luxury after a week of sleeping in a tent. I crawled into my snug little billet, pulled the down comforter up to my chin, and squirmed around, trying to position that annoying crossbar somewhere around my midsection. I missed Joeline sorely, but she needed to have the guest bed to herself. Looking out the window, I watched fireflies glow and disappear and was out in a flash.

I woke up the next morning to Joeline thumping into the room with her cane.

"Marty, my bandages are getting a little loose. Can you wrap them back up?" She sank onto the bed.

I sat up, still half asleep, and fumbled with the bandages on her arm. The sight of her black-and-blue skin made the room spin. I took a couple of deep breaths to shore up my weak intestinal fortitude and secured the bandaging around her arm.

"That oughta hold everything in place. Now what about your leg?" I gave it a quick once-over. "It's still wrapped up nice and tight."

"Thank goodness. You know, I could use a nice, hot shower."

"How are you going to do that without soaking your bandages?"

"Go get some trash bags and duct tape."

I found Frank in the kitchen putting on a pot of coffee. I asked for the requested items, and he promptly supplied them without question.

Back downstairs, I wrapped up Joeline's arm and leg, and we maneuvered into the shower and onto the bench. Hunched over, I fumbled around trying to help her get freshened up.

"I must look ridiculous in these garbage bags."

I leaned back and looked her up and down. "You look pretty good to me."

"Martin," she said, flushing a little.

"Joel, you're alive. You've never been more beautiful in your life."

I reached over to hug her. That type of gesture almost always invited some form of interruption. And there it was—the pounding on the door. "Mom and Dad, are you guys in there?"

I groaned. "At least they didn't barge in this time."

Our romantic interlude now vanished, I turned the water off, and we prepared for the next adventure: getting Joeline up to the first floor. A piggyback ride wasn't going to work. Using her cane, the handrail, and occasionally one of the kids, she managed to make it to the top.

As we settled her back onto the couch, I asked, "Now that you've had your morning workout, what can I get you for breakfast?"

"Pain pills."

"Now, honey, you've told me a million times not to take pills on an empty stomach. How 'bout some fluffy, apple pancakes? You've got to be famished."

She nodded and closed her eyes.

All the kids gathered in the family room to watch Saturday morning cartoons as I got to work whipping up yolks and batter while Frank fried up some sausage and authentic Canadian bacon. We had every burner on full flame, bacon grease splattering, flour flying, apple peeler whirling, and soon, the sink boasted an impressive collection of dirty dishes and utensils.

I was in the middle of flipping yet another apple-encrusted pancake when Loren came into the kitchen and took a seat at the counter.

"Hey, guys, I just talked to Dr. Lane. Listen to this."

It seemed that late the day before, the good doctor had performed surgery on a father and his son who had been hiking the trails in the back country around Banff when they happened upon a grizzly. They began backing away quietly, and when they thought they had retreated far enough, they began to hightail it south. Unfortunately, the bear was on the lookout for a high tail, and he bolted right after them in vigorous pursuit.

When the father heard the thunderous crashing of the approaching creature, he grabbed his little boy, dove to the ground, and rolled up around him in the fetal position, both of them frantically praying for the gift of long life.

"In the few seconds it took the bear to catch up to his prey," Loren said, "he apparently cooled off some. He gnawed on the father briefly and then turned to the son. I can't imagine how, but the two were able to remain motionless and silent the entire time."

Supposedly, according to what I'd read, when a grizzly sees its quarry lying down, prostrate on the ground, his aggression will diminish. No doubt, grizzlies everywhere appreciate the belief in this sentiment.

To not move or scream was an impressive feat, although they were most likely aided by the same physical phenomenon that assisted me in my bear encounters—paralysis. This may be the preferred state of being, considering grizzlies have the strongest front limbs of any animal in the world. One paw swipe can kill a moose. The fangs of an adult male are close to three inches long, and their nails can be twice that length. That hump on their back is one gigantic mass of muscle.

I knew all too well that bears had plucked hikers from trees, pulled campers from tents, or chased down backpackers in just a few strides, snapping off their limbs like twigs. I'd even heard of one encounter where a grizzly attacked a man and was then found sitting on his mangled corpse off in the woods.

"Believe it or not," Loren said, "the bear eventually got tired of them and ambled away. A couple of rangers heard them yelling for help and came to their rescue. The bear left some pretty serious teeth marks for Dr. Lane to sew up. But they lived to tell the tale."

And apparently they did.

I had to hand it to the rangers in that story. They were certainly at the right place at the right time. But sometimes rangers aren't at the right place, or at the right time.

One evening in Yosemite during our Wild West trip, Walt was busy doing the dinner dishes when he heard rustling behind some bushes. In a strange lapse of caution, he approached the bushes with a frying pan and began swooshing away.

This understandably upset the two teenage bears who simply wanted to dine on some fresh berries in peace. They lunged out from the side of the brush, and like the magician David Copperfield, Walt vanished into thin air, reappearing seconds later inside the van. We joined him in the vehicle, imitating his baseball swings with the frying pan, convulsing with laughter.

A ranger happened to be passing by and, observing all the commotion, called a colleague who arrived several minutes later in a heavily equipped pickup truck. By that time, the bears had meandered off into the hills right behind our site. To our surprise, the rangers geared themselves up and darted off in hot pursuit. Things soon quieted down, and we slid into our sleeping bags inside the van for safety.

About an hour later, a horrendous racket woke us all up. The bears had returned and were now inside the rangers' truck, having a ball absolutely pillaging it. Yogi and his sidekick Boo-Boo were throwing things out the back of the truck, growling and almost barking in laughter as they looked for that elusive picnic basket.

We sat huddled in our van, still and quiet, listening to the clanging and clattering. All of the National Park Service's literature states "Do not disturb bears in their natural habitat," so we dutifully honored those guidelines.

The rangers must have been pretty embarrassed when they returned to their truck. They didn't even bother to ask us for a report. They just slunk away into the darkness, presumably trying to conjure up some believable explanation for their supervisor.

That afternoon Frank suggested we take the kids on an outing to give our wives some peace and quiet. Joeline was now propped up on the couch dozing. With Loren's help, Julie started a load of our camping laundry. She had insisted on staying behind to help the convalescents.

The rest of us took off to the site of the Calgary 1988 Winter Olympics, held six years prior. The bobsled run, luge run, and ski jumping area were all still intact and operational.

At the ski jumping structure, we must have climbed a thousand steps to get to the top. My heart was pounding when we got there—and not just from the exercise. I had always wanted to see what the "agony of defeat" looked like, facing down into the valley of death, and indeed, it is startling. A combination of terrifying and shocking.

I've done a few scary things in my life: jumped out of airplanes, rappelled down sheer rock faces, water-skied standing on a chair balanced on a disk, snorkeled with sharks, and flown a hundred feet through the air on a motorcycle.

But how could anyone ever get up the nerve to careen down one of these launch pads, be hurled recklessly through the atmosphere, all the while struggling mightily to maintain enough balance to keep from landing face-first on a rock-hard surface going about sixty miles an hour?

If I could total up all the nerve I expended in my youth, I still wouldn't have enough to plunge down a ski jump.

Though the venue was still operational, it was August, a month not known for record-setting snow conditions. No athletes were there to display nerves of steel. So we returned to the house to prepare dinner.

Frank was cooking a pork roast, and I joined in by peeling half the potatoes in the Northern Hemisphere. I don't even like potatoes.

Julie and Grace announced they were going horseback riding again. This spurred Mollie into action—if they were going horseback riding, by God so was she. The three of them ran off to Alice and Allin's barn. The neighbors would be returning with them for dinner.

Since Frank had to go back to work on Monday, Joeline and I agreed that we would depart then from Calgary. We didn't want to overstay our welcome. I had asked Joeline several more times if she wanted to fly home, but she said no.

"I'll need to start moving a bit over the next few days, and I'd rather do that with you guys than go home and be by myself. And it's so beautiful out here. I want to enjoy it as much as I can."

And I wanted to help her enjoy it as much as she could. With that goal in mind, I flipped through several of our travel books hoping to locate accommodations consisting of solid walls and hard floors to make things as comfortable for Joeline as possible—a hotel, or maybe a log cabin. Our backup plan was to continue to camp, a very likely scenario given that every permanent structure in all of Canada was occupied. We had a week left, and during that time, we had to slowly make our way southwest to Seattle for our flight back home to North Carolina.

I excused myself and went downstairs to use the phone. After an hour of calling every hotel and motel along our intended route and all the lodges in the park, I resigned myself to plan B. I put a call into the main office at Glacier. My mouth dropped when a ranger actually answered.

"If you arrive before midafternoon, I guarantee you'll find an open campsite, especially on a Monday."

Guarantee? I had a bad feeling about this guy. He must have been living under a rock all summer if he thought securing any campsite could be guaranteed.

"Would it be possible to reserve a site? We can prepay if that helps."

"Nope, sorry. We don't handle any reservations at the park grounds."

"Could you transfer me to someone who does?"

"Nope, sorry, sir, the main office is closed on Saturdays. But like I said, you'll have no problem getting a campsite on a Monday. Have a good day now."

What a waste of time.

Oh my God. It was Saturday, and I told Seth I'd call him on Friday. *You know what? Screw it.* After everything that had happened, IBM just wasn't all that important right now. It would have to wait.

I returned upstairs to assist with any last-minute dinner preparations. Frank had everything under control, so I checked in with Joeline, who said she felt well enough to join us for dinner. I helped her to the table and called the little guys.

The older girls came bursting through the door giddy with excitement from their ride, Allin and Alice following closely behind. Allin waltzed in with two pies, one in each hand, held up at shoulder height. He paraded them around the kitchen before ceremoniously placing them ever so gently on the counter.

"Those are some of the best-looking pies I've ever laid eyes on," I said.

He thrust out his chest. "I picked every last berry myself and baked them from scratch."

"What kind of berries are we talking here?"

"Saskatoons. And there's rhubarb too."

"What's a saskatoon?"

"You're in for a treat, my friend." Allin beamed. "Just one of the most delicious little fruits you have ever tasted."

Judging from the perfectly browned and rumpled contours of the crusts, Allin must have majored in patisserie. I scrutinized both pies. Would the crust be as good as my great-aunt Beeba's? God rest her soul. Or as good as Joeline's, to whom Beeba had bequeathed the skill?

Allin and Alice's arrival—specifically the arrival of their pies— lifted my spirits in one fell swoop. There isn't a dish in the whole world that tickles my tongue like a fresh, home-baked pie. Especially the sour fruit kind. While I wasn't sure about the saskatoons, you couldn't get any more sour than rhubarb.

We thanked Alice and Allin profusely for taking our girls horse-back riding and then dug in to our meal. The pork roast was out-standing, and the potatoes were some of the best ever peeled. But I hardly ate any of it because I was focused on those pies. I don't re-member what we talked about. I don't think I spoke a single word. I just pushed the food around aimlessly on my plate. I kept looking over at the pies, my eyes burning holes in them.

Joeline elbowed me, with her good arm, and whispered, "Cut it out. You've got pie eyes."

All I heard was "Cut it out." Sounded like something you should do to a pie.

As the time approached to indulge in dessert, my palms got sweaty, my throat dry, my stomach full of butterflies. How would a saskatoon-rhubarb pie taste? More importantly, how much could I eat without being rude?

The main course finally ended. I stared down at my lap, hoping to deter any conversation that would delay serving up the final course. My mission seemed lost as everyone kept talking. But Adam, God love him, said, "Loren, why don't we start carving up one of those pies?"

Ah! At long last, Loren placed a piece of pie in front of me. I paused for a moment, gazing in admiration. I reflected on what was about to happen. Fork in left hand, knife in right, I nudged the exquisite slice gently, touching both sides to exact its texture, to extract a bit of aroma. And then—I dove in.

I don't usually eat pie with two utensils, but this was different. This work of art demanded all the dexterity I could muster. And the pie melted in my mouth. I reveled at every delectable bite, nibbling on each splendid fragment slowly to prolong the enjoyment. Time seemed to stand still.

While I savored the last bite of this masterpiece, my wandering eyes locked on the lone wedge of pie left stranded in the pan on the counter. My college studies had familiarized me with a famous German axiom that now came to mind: "Das Bier, das nicht getrunken wird, hat seinen Beruf verfehlt," or roughly, "The beer that isn't consumed has missed its calling." Substitute pie for beer, and you have it.

I was agonizing for one more sweet berry, one last nibble of the bitter rhubarb. The internal struggle was monstrous, but I resolved to restrain myself. *Do not ask for it! Hope like hell they offer, but don't ask.*

Everyone stayed at the table chit-chatting. Except me, of course. I was fixated on that last piece of pie. An eon went by before Loren finally brought it up.

"I'm way too full," she said. "How about you, Frank?"

No, he didn't want it either—a little too tangy for him.

I was almost insulted. How could he not want it?

Loren continued around the table.

Alice sighed. "I ate too many potatoes."

Joeline gazed into my pitiful, pleading eyes and quickly passed. Lucky for me, she has always preferred apple.

Now it was down to two of us.

"Allin," Loren said, "did you save room for the last piece?"

"I always have room for pie." He chuckled.

I gasped. That was *my* line.

Loren must have thought that because Allin had labored for hours picking the berries, he ought to have first dibs. And Allin had obviously forgotten that I was the guest.

I struggled pitifully to choke back my disappointment.

Certainly Loren would say, "And, Marty, would you like a little more of this delicious pie? We can always cut into the second one."

That would not only get me another slab of pie, but also decrease the risk of them taking the second pie home with them, thereby increasing my chances of consuming the entire thing later when no one was looking.

But those words never came, and in a final act of torment, that last piece of scrumptious pie was served up to the person sitting right next to me. I had to sit there politely, acting like a normal person, ignoring the sweet aroma wafting past my nostrils, while Allin gobbled it down.

We sat around for an hour or two in the living room and had a lovely conversation. I think. I was still thoroughly distracted. The remaining pie sat in the other room emitting a mouthwatering scent able to fracture a man's soul. Maybe we would have some later in the night.

About eleven o'clock, Allin said it was time for them to head home. They had an early start Sunday morning. He and Alice were truly nice people, and I hated to see the evening end. Especially without another serving of pie.

As we all stood to walk them to the door, Loren said, "Adam, your pie was amazing, as always. Thank you so much. Why don't you take the second one back home with you?"

What? No way!

Tears came to my eyes. This was my last chance. The pie was heading out of the house forever if I didn't act quickly.

In desperation, I blurted out something like, "Yes! Allin that pie was amazing! One of the best I've ever had. Thank you so much." I laid it on thick. "You were right. Saskatoons are delicious little berries. You know, they don't grow those down in North Carolina."

But everyone was far too nice to perceive the malice behind my platitudes, mistaking them as sincere compliments. My mind raced to concoct one last inane attempt to rescue that pie. I came up empty-handed. Figuratively—and literally.

Alice and Allin bid us all a fond farewell and a safer journey home—and walked out into the night with that glorious creation.

17.

on the road again

Glacier National Park, Montana.
Left to right: Grace, Max, Mollie, Angela, Julie, and me.

Two days later, I stared at the back of the van, not eager to pack up and leave the Walshes' hospitality or any chance of having another piece of pie. Nor was I looking forward to reuniting with my air mattress, even with the trusty Silly Putty plastered in place. But Joeline and I remained firm about taking off that morning.

I was shoving in a duffel bag, avoiding the damp patch on the carpet courtesy of our soggy firewood, when Frank came up next me. Dressed in a suit and tie, he extended his hand. "We loved having you, and you can certainly stay longer if that'll help."

As tempting as that was, it was time for us to go. There's an apt old saying, "Guests, like fish, begin to smell after three days." It was beginning to smell like day four.

"Frank, y'all have been a godsend to us. I truly don't know what we would have done. But we need to get out of your hair now and make our way back south."

He gave me as firm a handshake as I could handle. "Come back and visit us anytime and stay in touch."

I watched his car wind down the driveway and then turned around and nearly tripped over Grace.

"What's that around your neck?" I asked.

"It's my sweatshirt." She tied it tighter. "Smells like a horse." She took a big whiff. "I'm never washing it again. Can we please, please stay a couple more days? Or could you just leave me here?"

As I was giving this due consideration, Max burst out of the house and started running around the van. "Dad, can we get some more doughnuts?"

"Cool it with the doughnuts!" Maybe it was a good thing we were leaving, especially after what had happened the day before at church. I blamed myself for not monitoring the kids more carefully. Sure, they loved getting doughnuts after the service, but did they have to turn into piranhas, swarming in and devouring everything in sight? And that was on top of us arriving late (as usual), nearly flattening a nun in the parking lot, and then disrupting the entire service.

Julie came out clutching Joeline's bag of leftover Thai food from the prior evening out with the Walshes. When I told Frank and Loren that we wanted to express our gratitude by taking them to their favorite restaurant, how was I to know they would choose my least favorite food.

I had eaten at a Thai restaurant only once before. More precisely, I had sat in one for a couple of hours, dismembering the foreign fare occupying my plate into small enough segments to appear partially ingested. At least last night, I was able to force down half a spring roll to be polite.

"All right, everyone in."

I closed Joeline's passenger door gingerly, being careful not to whack her bad arm or leg, or to crinkle her sundress. She had managed to put it on without any help. I took a moment to admire the Walshes' house and their spectacular view one last time.

What were the chances that Joeline would get paired up with a roommate who would rescue our entire family? Was there any explanation other than divine intervention? I had never put much stock into angels. But the Walshes' timely lifeline and the couple at Emerald Lake were making me think twice.

We rolled down the driveway, and I peered into the rearview mirror. The Walsh kids were jumping up and down waving goodbye.

I turned onto the road wondering if we would ever see them again.

We were about to get onto the freeway heading south when Joeline remembered we needed ice for the cooler. So we pulled over at a gas station to handle that issue. Right afterward, the kids started begging for doughnuts—like they hadn't had enough at church. We stopped for that necessity and reembarked once more, only to circle back a third time for milk.

As we stumbled out of the grocery store, a light bulb flashed in my head. We needed oil!

Returning to the store, I found only a couple of cans of kerosene stuck at the back of a bottom shelf. But no oil.

I called over to the attendant, "I can't find any lamp oil. Is kerosene the same thing?" That was something I probably should have known.

"Sure is," he said. "But I wouldn't use it in your lanterns, especially anywhere around your campsite. Smoke'll make you sick."

"Hmm. That's not good. Does anybody else around here carry oil?"

"Nope, not as I reckon. No, sir."

Okay. From now on, only lanterns that use batteries, the long-lasting kind.

All in all, we spent three hours shopping our way down to the international border. As we approached our homeland, I explained to the kids that they had to be on their best behavior when we were inspected by the border guards. The girls, seemingly unfazed by my warning, were carrying on laughing and giggling, even as we pulled up to the guard shack. When they noticed the car in front of us being waved off to the side and several sizable, ornery-looking guards coming out to inspect it, they suddenly clammed up. Everyone was sufficiently frightened, especially me, but we passed right through.

Right through to the duty-free shop, that is.

I have great difficulty passing duty-free shops without investing in some free duty. And invest I did, although over the years, customs had curtailed the allowed amount of investment from one gallon to one liter. When I returned to the States from Europe a couple of decades earlier, you could bring a gallon of booze with you, and rest assured, I brought a gallon with me.

I shelled out my last wad of Canadian dollars in exchange for the booze and went to use the restroom. There was a substantial line outside the women's room, even here, in the middle of nowhere at the Montana border.

As I exited the men's room, Grace tugged on my arm and whispered, "Dad, guard the door. I'm going in the men's. What the heck are those women doing in there anyway that takes so long! Stand right here. Okay?"

"Certainly." Admiring her initiative, I diligently guarded the door.

She wasn't very quick about her business either, and before long, the women's line had totally dissipated, as had all other patrons in the vicinity. Seeing as there was no longer anything to guard from, I sauntered back to the van, feeling my sentry duty was complete.

Everyone piddled around a bit, waiting for Grace. What the heck was she doing in there? Finally, a bit annoyed, I went back to the men's room and knocked on the door.

"Um, Grace. Everything okay? We'd really like to get back on the road."

"I can't get out!" she yelled.

"What do you mean you can't get out?"

"The door is stuck! I keep pulling, but nothing's happening."

Oh God, not again. My women were sure having their difficulties in northerly washrooms.

"Get me outta here!" she yelled.

I joked to Grace, "I'm glad you didn't try to climb out the window."

"Dad," she said sarcastically, "there's no window in here, and even if there was, I'd never climb out of the men's room." She paused. "Maybe the women's, but definitely not the men's."

In fact, Grace had hidden quietly in the bathroom because she didn't want anyone to hear her girl's voice calling for help from a men's room. Poor Grace was mortified, and I had unwittingly deserted her.

I used all my body weight to smash the door open, providing far more heft than was actually required for the task.

"Okay, Grace. Let's get going," I said, rubbing my aching shoulder.

"I can't go out now, after all that noise. Someone will see me."

So I went in, wrapped my jacket around her, and came out shielding her from view. It turned out, though, that because Grace was as skinny as a rail and I was considerably wider than a rail, she was sufficiently hidden. But, no matter, there wasn't anyone within eyeshot of us.

Everyone now finally loaded up in the van, it was time to officially cross the border and pick up my duty-free booty. The cashier had instructed us to stop just across the border to retrieve the goods. So we crossed countries, and I began cranking my head around in every direction trying to locate the place where I was supposed to pick up my packages.

But I was having no luck. I had expected to see a building or a shack or something. I began to feel pretty stupid, again. What a great scam this could be. They knew I would be too embarrassed to go back and demand a refund. And I couldn't go back across the border anyway, at least not easily. I'd have to go through US Customs and back into the Canadian Customs. I could just picture it.

"And how long was your visit to the United States, sir?"

"Um, about three minutes."

"Okay, and just what is the purpose of your return visit?"

"I'm back to pick up some duty-free booty."

"Lock him up, Fred."

Just as I was getting a little miffed about all this, a little bitty car sped up to us, two bottles were handed out the window, and then it sped back toward Canada. The bottles securely in hand, I cruised down the road, a big smile on my face, a small thirst brewing on my insides, acting like I never doubted a thing.

A few miles later, we came across something we hadn't seen since we'd left the States—the legendary American road crew. This group had ten men, one guy wielding a shovel, eight guys leaning on shovels watching the first guy, and one guy supervising. It was great to be back home.

Within a half hour, we were at the eastern entrance to Glacier National Park. Visibility was so poor that you couldn't even see the base of the mountains. When I pulled up to the park booth, the ranger slid his window open, looked up at the sky, and said, "Yep, those clouds just rolled in overnight and we're expecting 'em to stick around for three or four days." He grinned, somehow thinking it was funny. "Hope you brought your rain gear."

"That's fantastic." I didn't expect anything less. But weather was the least of my concerns at this point. "I'm a little nervous about getting a campsite. We're almost out of gas, and what's with all the construction?"

"Oh, nothing to worry about. You've got plenty of time to get gas and do a little sightseeing before you head to the campground." He handed a leaflet out the window. "Here's a park map. Hope y'all have a nice time. Stay dry!" He slid his window shut.

"Uh-huh." I slowly drove away and then stopped at the nearest gas station, positive I was going to regret my decision. We filled up the tank, used the facilities yet again, and raced off to find a campsite.

Back on the main road, we breezed ahead about fifty yards before coming to a dead standstill at the end of a long line of cars. Road construction. Amassing speed was not something we excelled at. We were much better at amassing delays.

"Good Lord," Joeline said. "This isn't happening."

"No, it's not, dear. You heard what the good ranger told us—we've got plenty of time," I said with as much bitter sarcasm as I could invoke.

We inched along for roughly thirty minutes before crawling into Rising Sun Campground. I was just about ready to shoot myself when a frumpy campground ranger peered out of his little shack. "Sorry, sir. The campground filled up just about twenty minutes ago."

What a sick sense of humor this guy had, toying with me like that. It wasn't funny. I studied his face. He wasn't kidding.

Luckily my stockpile of anger was depleted. I could only feel apathy. "I'm sure it did. Say, would you mind if we drove through just to have a look?"

"Be my guest." He waved us in.

I had no ulterior motive in asking other than perhaps to torture myself and to delay making a decision about where to go next. I meandered slowly through the camp, looking at all the happily pitched tents, wondering how on a late, wet Monday morning so many people were still there. Didn't they have somewhere to go?

What a minute! Was I seeing what I thought I was seeing? I slammed on the brakes.

"What is that?" I said to Joeline, pointing.

"An empty site?" she said dryly.

"Yeah." I wasn't sure what to make of it, so we kept going. Again, I slammed on the brakes, this time throwing the van into reverse. I screeched to a backward halt directly in front of a second empty site.

"And what the hell is that?" I shouted, with a touch of vindication.

"Uh, looks like another empty site."

"That's it. Everyone out of the van!" I went around to open the side door. The kids began unloading one by one. "Not you, Angela, you stay with us. Julie, you and Grace go back to that empty site over there." I waved them off to the first empty site. "Mollie and Max, you stay at this one. Your mom and I are going to have a word with the ranger. Hold these spots."

I got back into the van, both ecstatic and furious. It was probably just an oversight, but what would we have done if I hadn't requested a brief gander through the campground? We would have driven off to God knows where and spent the entire day trying desperately to find accommodations when there were two perfectly good sites right here.

Well, to be frank, "good" wasn't the most appropriate adjective. In fact, it was pretty obvious why these two sites were still empty. They were probably the two most undesirable sites in the entire campground, maybe the entire country. One was the size of a handicapped parking spot and bordering along the road. The second one was hemmed in and crushed between three other sites.

"I just don't get it," I said to Joeline as we drove back to the campground entrance.

"What? Why a park ranger would lie about empty campsites? Maybe because they're so awful."

"Okay, that too. But, no. What I don't get is this." I made a sweeping motion with my hand to point out the landscape in front of us, what little of it was visible. "Our parks are located in the most beautiful, panoramic areas in this country. Hundreds of thousands of acres and forests and mountains—" my arms flailed in the air—"and they stick us in this tiny, pissant hole here—"

"Martin, would you please keep your hands on the steering wheel?"

"Right, sorry. But why are these campgrounds so horrendously laid out? What idiot builds a campsite right on the road? Why would you cram four sites directly on top of one another like that? How about a little privacy? I don't want to sing 'Kumbaya' with our neighbors."

Luckily I had an inkling that yelling at the ranger might not be in our best interest, no matter how many empty, ill-placed spots he was unaware of. Frumpy apologized profusely, admitting confusion on his part, and granted us permission to occupy whichever site we preferred. Joeline chose the second site, figuring that although we'd be squeezed in like sardines, at least none of our kids would become speed bumps.

I asked Frumpy if he could kindly direct us to the firewood.

"Right over yonder. Five dollars a parcel."

"You mean it's not complimentary?"

He gave me an empty look.

"It's free in Canada. Just something to consider. We'll take two bundles."

Over to the firewood bin I went. Five dollars a bundle, huh? A very small bundle. Really, not even a bundle—more like a handful. Literally burning money. All those hard-earned, hand-chopped logs, all that free Canadian timber—still so damp it would take a blow torch to light anything.

We returned to our site, collecting kids along the way, grateful to have a place for the night. I pitched the tent in a somber, but admittedly relieved, mood. Then I moved on to the canopy. With bad weather in the forecast, we would need to haul it out for the first time and use it to cover the picnic table.

Because setting up this apparatus was such a chore, I didn't get it out unless it was absolutely necessary. The cubic footage required to house the contents of the box was greater than the volume provided by the box. Scrunching the canvas, poles, ropes, and pegs into this tiny little box in the first place must have been a closely guarded trade secret. Getting all this stuff back into the box required a master's degree in geometric engineering.

After removing all the contents, I discovered that the center pole was missing, rendering the whole contraption useless. Seriously? But given our trip to that point, how could I possibly be surprised? On the bright side, I could now simply dispose of the entire passel of parts without any repacking.

It was getting toward midafternoon, and though the sky was still dolefully overcast, the youngins needed to get out and partake in some sort of physical activity. I opened the floor for suggestions.

"Let's go to a waterfall!" Angela said, jumping up and down.

"That would be my first choice," Joeline said.

The others nodded in agreement.

I examined the map and spotted some squiggly vertical lines indicating a waterfall just up the road. It looked like a short hike through the woods that Joeline might be able to navigate. And we could check out the nearby gorge on the way. This time, I would bring my camera, not about to repeat what had happened at Maligne Canyon.

In keeping with my photographic fortunes, the Sunrift Gorge turned out to be about eight feet deep, twenty-five feet long, and about ten feet across. Not so much a gorge, as a trench. A very big trench maybe, but not a gorge. I never even took the lens cap off.

A little farther down the road, at Baring Falls, Grace and Max led the charge. The trail turned out to be too strenuous for Joeline, especially since the light drizzle made the ground slippery, so she returned to the trailhead. The rest of us continued on down, and just past the footbridge, we caught sight of the falls. It wasn't nearly as impressive as the others we'd seen on the trip. Given the weather, Joeline's condition, and the bleak sights, I regretted not remaining at the campground—or with the Walshes.

To add some excitement to this underwhelming excursion, I descended to the base of the falls and began working my way across the stream, hopping from one boulder to another. As expected, I slipped and plunged my lower half into the ice-cold water. Now, my only pair of shoes were soaking wet, along with a significant portion of my pants.

I tried not to let on that I had probably smashed my leg in half. That would be easy because I'd injured my leg so often over the years, I walked around with a limp most of the time anyway. People would notice if I *didn't* limp.

Gathering as much composure as possible in this embarrassing and painful predicament, I said to my much-amused children, "Maybe we should all work our way back and see how Mom is doing."

I lumbered along, trying to disguise my new limp as my usual limp. Joeline eyed me suspiciously as we came off the trail.

At the parking lot, I noticed a large, squared-off rock nestled right next to the van. I stepped back a few feet, admiring the huge stone from top to bottom. That baby would make for a sturdy seat at our campfire. It would sure beat balancing on our wobbly logs, especially with a busted leg. I hoisted the boulder up, twisted around, and let it slam down in the back of the van—proceeding to snap something in my lower lumbar region.

How was I going to hide this new calamity? A wrenched back is more difficult to conceal than a broken leg. With all my grunting and groaning, and bending over at a forty-five-degree angle, it was pretty obvious what I had done.

Joeline stared at me in disbelief, mumbling as she contorted herself into the van. She shot me one of those looks no man ever wants to receive. Translation: "You're on your own now, buddy."

I shuffled over to the driver's seat and scooched in, mounting a supreme effort to refrain from further whimpering. Since I was more or less molded into the sitting position, I made an executive decision and announced that we'd be driving through the park to see the sights. Yes, those sights that weren't at all visible in the vaporous gloom. This would give me time to partially recover from my self-induced afflictions and to ponder how I might get myself and my new furniture out of the van once we returned to the campsite.

"You do realize the only sight we're going to see is more fog," Joeline said.

"Maybe it'll clear up."

18.

the valley of death

About to hike the Grand Canyon, Arizona, 1972.
Left to right: Couzy, Mel, Walt, Woody, and me.

Things remained uncomfortably quiet in the van as we drove back to the campsite through what might as well have been a gargantuan cotton ball. After I situated Joeline at our picnic table, I was faced with the onerous task of removing the boulder from the back of the van. Normally, this wouldn't be as difficult as putting it into the van, but circumstances had changed.

I contorted myself into an awkward squat, trying to use my good leg for propulsion, and then gave a mighty heave to the rock and hoisted it not quite an inch. After taking a multitude of baby steps to cover the fifteen feet to the campfire pit, I dropped my payload, making sure I was leaning forward when I let go.

The boulder plunged straight down, as they usually do, and caught the very tips of my soaking wet gym shoes. If I had been wearing my old faithful industrial boots, the damn rock would have bounced right off. Instead, I was pinned to the ground, frantically trying to keep from falling over backward. My left shoe quickly pulled loose, but the other one stayed firmly entrenched. Now able to balance on my good leg, I managed to pull my right foot out of the trapped shoe and wiggle my toes, relieved they were all still there and operable.

I assembled the available troops to help me rock the boulder back and forth. After several heave-hoes, we were able to budge the boulder approximately one millimeter and extract my flattened shoe—much more preferable than extracting a flattened foot.

Freed from my hobble, I slapped together some salami sandwiches and laid out a handful of kettle chips for Joeline. Her addiction to chips is akin to mine for pie, and it was a testament to her exhaustion that she could eat only one or two. Our five little dervishes assisted by sucking up every last crumb.

I had no idea how we would get Joeline into the tent, especially given my rigid upright position, but the time had come to cross that bridge. I asked for volunteers, and the older girls rallied into self-appointed positions. Grace and Mollie flattened the lip to the tent so Joeline wouldn't have to lift her leg over the threshold, and then Julie and I helped her stoop down through the tent door. All four of us lowered her onto the sleeping bag we had placed on top of my air mattress. Switching bedding with her was the least I could do to help her sleep comfortably. She hadn't minded the thinner blow-up mattress, but it would be my buffer from Mother Earth for the rest of the trip.

Once Joeline was horizontal and snuggled, Max zipped the bag around her, being careful not to touch her injuries. Mission accomplished. But we probably wouldn't remember how we did it come the next night.

I ushered the little campers out of Big Blue to give Joeline a reasonable shot at getting off to sleep. Julie, Grace, and Mollie built up a small woodpile in the fire circle, Max doused it with lighter fluid, and I threw in a dozen matches. In seconds, we had a splendid blaze going.

The kids sat comfortably on their logs, marshmallows drooping precariously off the ends of their sticks, inches away from combusting into sugarcoated fireballs. Max had two marshmallows affixed to his limber stick, and when they simultaneously burst into flames, he began gleefully whirling his stick around trying to put out the fire. Before I could issue a warning, one of the Molotov cocktails flew off his stick and soared just inches past Mollie's face.

Mollie's eyes bulged in terror, and Max bent over in laughter.

"All right, that's it," I said as forcefully as I could without disturbing Joeline. "Max, you almost set Mollie on fire!" I limped over to stamp out the detonated goo grenade, still smoldering in the gravel, thankful that I wasn't extinguishing my daughter.

"All sticks will remain entirely inside the fire circle from now on. When your marshmallow is done, pull the stick out slowly. Never whip it out, especially if your marshmallow is on fire."

Christ Almighty, couldn't we go more than ten minutes without some life-threatening crisis?

No one said a word. I looked down longingly at my boulder. After all my effort, it would have provided the perfect perch to rest my weary body and mind, except that I couldn't physically lower myself onto it. So I stood there while everyone finished their s'mores.

"I think it's time y'all hit the hay. And be very quiet. Don't wake up your mother."

The girls made a big show of setting their sticks down inside the designated fire circle and then disappeared into Big Blue while Max and I set off for the bathroom.

After completing our nighttime routine, we exited the facilities and were immediately accosted by a dozen thunderous Harleys circling the campground. Their cannonade rattled every tent in the area, and their long string of headlights lit up the forest canopy above us.

We stood still until the last biker had passed and then began following tentatively in their tracks back to our site. As their rumbling faded into the distance, so did their illumination, and we were steeped in darkness, our dying flashlight providing only a dim light through the dense foliage. Max reached out and fumbled for my hand.

"Dad, I can't see anything. The batteries are running out."

"We'll be okay. We're almost back."

"No we aren't! We need to hurry."

"Max, my main man, many years ago, way before you were born, I hiked through the Grand Canyon when it was a lot darker than this. I didn't even have a dying flashlight."

"You did? How could you see where you were going?"

"I couldn't. In fact I almost didn't make—" Maybe I shouldn't be telling him this. "Anyway, it was very, very dark, but I eventually made it to the campground that night deep in the canyon."

We trudged forward into a consuming darkness that had us proceeding just below glacial speed—so slowly that had we bumped into a tree we wouldn't have even felt it.

"And see, Max? We made it too. Look, there's our tent. Head on in. We'll get some batteries tomorrow. I'll be in after I douse out the fire."

He fumbled around, trying to delay his departure, but eventually gave in and crawled through the portal into Big Blue. I grabbed some water and shuffled over to my boulder, still wishing I could bend over far enough to sit on it. I stared down into the glowing embers, thinking about that night in the canyon. One day I would tell Max the whole story. When he was older.

Our Wild West route took us along the North Rim of the Grand Canyon, so we figured that since it was there, we might as well go hike it. Our provisions consisted of some peanuts, 3 Musketeers bars, raisins, and a couple of paper-thin bedrolls. I filled a gallon milk jug with cool water and stuck my old, beat-up camera in my pocket. Several of us peeled off our shirts, despite ample signage advising against doing so, and headed down the fourteen-mile North Kaibab Trail, the only trail going from the North Rim all the way to the Colorado River.

We left behind the aspen trees and cool air and descended all too quickly into a furnace. The scenery was decidedly bland: dirt, sand, gravel, a zigzagging lizard, and more dirt. No matter, we couldn't take our eyes off the trail for more than a second for fear of plummeting off the edge. On top of that, the first two and a half miles of the trail were so steep we practically free-fell forward. I took off sprinting, pounding away like a runaway elephant on the hard rock path. A mile later, it felt like someone had driven a five-inch nail into the side of my left knee. I had to walk sideways to reduce the pain.

At noon, we arrived at Roaring Springs, just under the five-mile marker. Following Mel's lead, we all got buck-naked and jumped into the springs. The water was freezing cold, and we drank it by the handful—and I replenished the lukewarm water in my jug.

We continued to follow the path along the stream to Cottonwood Meadows, where an hour later, we jumped into the water again. The sun beat down on us like hellfire as we ate our melted candy bars. We stashed our skinny bedrolls under some rocks to use later that night—if we survived the hike all the way to the Colorado River and subsequently returned to these meadows.

The heat intensified as we trudged along the baking, barren canyon floor, slowing our pace to a virtual crawl. Our scorched eyes were too weary to process the foreboding beauty of the ancient landscape around us. I was dying a miserable, parched death, marooned in a sunken oven. My knee would not bend at all now.

Blisters started popping out on the backs of my heels from hiking crablike through the canyon. It felt as if someone had sliced off the bottom quarter of my feet and filled my shoes with pebbles. Pouring water over my burning body was no longer keeping me cool—I didn't feel sunburned as much as I felt charred. The only thing that kept us going forward was the uselessness of stopping.

Any pleasure I could have derived from this adventure was completely eclipsed by the knowledge that a return to the rim would be required. With a sick feeling, I knew that hiking out would be far worse than hiking in.

Six hours after setting off, we stumbled one by one into the Phantom Ranch, a rustic camp of ten or so cabins alongside the Colorado River. Walt and I trudged over to Bright Angel Creek and dropped in, hoping for the slightest bit of relief. But the only relief we got was when we scrambled out of the scorching water.

A few moments later, Mel emerged from the trail with a sunken face and glazed eyes. He stumbled into the creek, surprising us all by forgoing his normal strip-down. His muscles tightened, and he fell face-first into the water and sank lifelessly under the current. We watched his body convulse for a moment before mustering the strength to drag him to the shore.

Luckily, the three of us were in pretty good physical condition, although right then there was no visual evidence to support that claim. After Mel regained control of his faculties, we paid a visit to the canteen and drank their entire supply of lemonade and consumed an unnatural number of hot dogs.

I stopped one of the roaming rangers. "Excuse me, sir, can you direct me to the closest heliport?"

He laughed. "There actually is a heliport down here."

"I know. I'll pay whatever it takes."

"Well, it's ghastly expensive for private use, and besides, it's only open for emergencies."

"This is an emergency."

He laughed again. "You don't look like our typical emergency. But you might become an emergency if you're not careful." He squinted and examined me closer, then glanced down at the empty milk jug in my hand. His face turned grimly serious. "You know, son, at least twenty people die in this canyon every year. Some from heat stroke, some from dehydration, and some just fall right off the cliffs." Then he added soberly, "Most of the deaths are associated with some form of poor judgment."

My buddies and I were prime candidates to become five more statistics.

I chugged another lemonade and hiked the additional few hundred yards to cross over the Colorado River. It was an amazing feat of nature—both the river and the fact that I had enough energy to do it. I was so tired I had no appreciation for any of it. After snapping a few pictures from the south bank, I traversed back over the bridge to join the others.

Staggering our departures, Woody left around seven, Couzy and Mel closer to seven-thirty, while Walt and I finally mustered the energy around eight. We needed to return to the meadows for our gear, but we'd also agreed unanimously that to avoid repeating the torturous ordeal the next day, we should cover the relatively flat seven miles back to Cottonwood Meadows that night. That would leave the final seven-mile trek up and out for daybreak.

I filled my gallon jug and began plugging along toward our midnight haven. Walt was in considerable pain from the bleeding blisters on his feet, and I had phantom nails sticking out of my knees. Two miles of slow going through the canyon as it got dark—fast. We had to stop several times to adjust blister wrappings. Someone had told Walt that his ROTC boots would make great hiking apparel, the assumption being that he had worn them for years, when in fact, he was breaking them in that day, or rather, they were breaking him.

As the trail wound slightly up the canyon wall, the sound of the river fell gradually away. We were trying to stay close together, saying stupid things like "Why in the hell did we do this?" partly to keep track of each other, but mainly because we were really wondering why.

A couple of hours later, it had grown so dark in the canyon I couldn't tell if my eyes were open or shut without touching my eyelids. And yet I could see the bazillion stars blazing away in the sky and just the faintest glimmer of moonlight glistening on the uppermost sliver of the canyon rim, though neither provided a single photon of light down on the desert floor.

We continued our forward progress into oblivion, climbing up through a narrow part of the steep trail, when out of nowhere, like a nuclear bomb, we heard and felt a deafening explosion no more than fifty feet in front of us. A blast of air rushed past, and particles of something stung our faces and arms. I was so startled I almost fell off the trail.

Then it went completely quiet. We were immersed again in total silence, along with total blindness.

"What the hell was that?" Walt said.

Both of us stood there frozen, not moving a muscle, expecting and fearing that any second something else would slam down or shoot out of the night and sweep us away.

Several minutes passed. We couldn't very well stand there petrified all night. We reached out to touch each other, making sure neither of us had somehow dissolved away. Then we uttered a few soft syllables, seeing if we could evoke some sort of response from the impact site. Nothing happened, so we started inching forward, expecting eventually to come upon a smoldering mound of rubble, or bodies, or some sort of residue from the blast.

But we never did. With the two of us plodding along side by side on that narrow trail, we couldn't possibly have missed anything big enough to make the sound we heard and felt. And if whatever it was had rolled or fallen off the trail, we clearly would have heard it crashing farther down the cliffs.

We continued on for what seemed like forty days and forty nights, knees aching and feet throbbing, and plagued by the potential for another bomb in the blackness. The temperature dropped by twenty degrees, my water jug almost empty. The moon had risen almost to the canyon brim but our eyes were so dilated from the hours of darkness that we were practically squinting.

Walt and I finally stumbled into Cottonwood Meadows at about eleven-thirty. We found our bedrolls and collapsed onto the hard rocks.

The group got up around five the next morning to minimize our baking time and to delay meeting the perpetrator head on. Breaking camp didn't take long, because there was hardly anything to break. Breakfast didn't take long either, since we only had thirteen raisins left to split among the group.

Bringing a bite of nourishment along on a twenty-four-hour odyssey would have been a good idea, but someone needed to plan that. Since my friends and I were completely unencumbered by any tendencies towards good judgment, breakfast would have to wait for another day.

I filled up my plastic milk container with disturbingly warm water from Bright Angel Creek, hoping there were no animals upstream. Then we started the seven-mile trek out of the canyon.

The trail was stagnant and hot and torturous. After a couple of miles of gradual ascent, the path tilted ever upward, switchback after endless switchback, an arduous climb, thousands of feet of "straight up." The sunlight broke through early, sizzling the canyon walls hundreds of feet above us. Its burning rays edged ever lower as we inched ever higher, destined to meet at some broiling point in the middle.

It was incongruous—insane, really—that I was killing myself with the specific intent to ascend into what would hasten my skewering in this fiery pit. My poor shriveled mind was racing wildly. Could I actually get out of here? And if I did, would my knee ever work right again? And we did this on purpose?

I began seeing things—figures floating above the trail, my great-grandfather peeking around a rock, water fountains spraying ice cold water across the path. What I didn't see were my buddies. They had moved ahead briskly and were now out of sight, including Walt. I didn't object to them leaving me behind. But the thought of toppling over on the trail and passing away all alone, deserted in the desert—would they even know?

A few last strides in the shade, and my ascent would meet with the sunlight's descent. Just around the next switchback, my immersion into the roasting sunbeams finally occurred. I had never before experienced what an intense enemy the sun could be. I had read about it in stories of Death Valley, the hottest place on earth, but it's hard to fully comprehend the scorching power of the sun until you're steeped in it.

As I trudged along, I glanced up occasionally, hoping to get a glimpse of the canyon rim, thinking that a sighting of my destination would lift my spirits. When it finally came into view, I wished it hadn't. I still had about a half mile to go, straight up.

By now, I could hardly bend my wounded knee, and I fell farther and farther behind the others. It got so bad that I could only drag on for about five minutes between breaks, which, in turn, became ever longer in duration. The wind whipped up the canyons and reminded me of opening an oven on Thanksgiving, except that the heat smelled less like turkey and more like hot burning sand and cacti.

Rounding one particularly steep switchback, I stumbled, throwing my weight onto my bad knee. It immediately buckled, sending me sideways down onto my butt. This made for a fairly soft, if painful, landing, on the very precipice of the turn. Glancing over my shoulder, I was able to see straight down, maybe a hundred feet, to scores of jagged rocks and many a flourishing cactus. I recalled the Phantom ranger's words about people dying in the canyon: "Some just fall right off the cliffs."

Somewhere around eleven o'clock, my milk jug long ago expended, I trudged up alongside a portly old lady, huffing and puffing, dragging her purse in the dirt. I began matching her stride for stride. When we stopped for a moment, she wheezed out that she had gone into the canyon that morning with her "stupid" husband but had wisely turned back.

You can imagine my added torture when I couldn't outpace this plump septuagenarian. Believe me, I was busting it with everything I had. I just couldn't shake her. I would pull ahead a couple of paces, but I'd have to pause to regain a little strength, and she'd blow past me, like a tortoise. Then I would marshal all my energy, drag my remains off the ground, and trudge after her.

This agonizing exchange continued until I lost her. More accurately, she lost me. She winked at me and disappeared up around a switchback.

No longer needing to keep up with her, I celebrated by enjoying a slightly more extended respite. Though the path had widened out and was now cooler and flatter, I still couldn't proceed more than a few tormented strides without a belabored breather. But the benches, which had been providing hiatus for my pitiful carcass, had long since disappeared. What derelict would need a place to rest so close to the top of the trail? But my need for them had only heightened.

Soon I struggled to simply put the heel of one foot in front of the toes of the other foot. Considering my size 14 shoes, I was still making some progress. But eventually, and semi-voluntarily, my bad knee buckled again and I collapsed straightforward. I probably looked like I had been wandering the Australian Outback, lost for weeks, toasted to oblivion. Several minutes must have passed before I was nudged awake by some hikers I had passed going down. They suggested I move from the middle of the trail.

I slowly regained my sensibilities, diminished as they had become. My life began passing before my eyes. Was this it? Was this all there was? If I was going to die on the Kaibab Trail, at least I'd be more dramatic about it. Fall off a steep cliff or get stampeded by a herd of rampaging mules. How about a rattlesnake bite? But certainly not face down in the dirt.

Two guys sporting Boston Red Sox caps passed and said I was only a hundred yards from the top. Spurred on by this knowledge, I mustered every ounce of vitality hidden away in the recesses of my anatomy and pushed on in one final, valiant assault.

Crushing exhaustion took control almost instantly. I began debating which of my dramatic exits I would choose when I spotted one of my buddies ahead of me. At least I thought it was a buddy. My vision was so blurred, it could have been a saguaro cactus. The thing trotted down the trail and escorted me back to the long-awaited parking lot. After eight hours of hiking, I collapsed against the trailhead sign while my trip mates, never so amused, doused me with boundless gallons of cool water—one swallow of which I would have killed for only an hour earlier.

Still in a daze, I asked, "How'd you know I was stuck down on the trail?"

They stopped laughing long enough to tell me, "Some hikers said they had passed a wretched-looking guy sleeping amid donkey droppings in the middle of the trail, about a half mile down." The story was subsequently confirmed by a troop of donkey riders. The boys figured it had to be me.

I remembered collapsing, but I didn't remember dozing off, nor did I remember a thing about donkeys—or their droppings. On top of that, I didn't remember anyone stopping to make sure I wasn't dead.

I never saw the old lady again either, bless her heart. I wanted to thank her for giving me the motivation to make it out.

While I was still in the throes of my recovery, some guy walked up to me. "You must be the guy I heard about lying on the trail. Can I take your picture?"

I could just see myself on the cover of *Backpacker* magazine. Headline: "The Canyon Claims Twenty-Fifth Victim This Year."

So I declined his offer, but he took my picture anyway.

Apparently our group had caused quite a commotion. Couzy and Woody had sprinted the last mile and a half to the parking lot amid cheers from a disbelieving crowd.

Anxious to wipe the donkey doo and sweat from my body, I tumbled into the van, and we drove to the showers. We invested a fortune in quarters, giving those showerheads a real workout.

The most unfortunate aspect to this entire adventure was that a well-planned hike to the bottom of the canyon could have been an incredibly gratifying experience—not a torturous one.

Yes, maybe someday I would tell Max the story of my near-death experience in the Grand Canyon. But then again, maybe I wouldn't.

19.

witless on whitney

Midnight hike down Mount Whitney, California, 1978.

I sped down Going-to-the-Sun Road, a gorgeous park thruway and the only road that traverses the entirety of Glacier Park. We pulled into the packed parking lot at the visitor center, and I nabbed a spot just as someone was pulling out—prompting the young driver from the other direction to display an elongated finger for my viewing pleasure.

The center was exploding with people. The clouds had parted that morning releasing the sun and what looked like every tourist within a hundred-mile radius. The three rangers manning the station were running around with their hands on their heads, barely able to scratch the surface of the swelling throng's needs. Red-faced, sweaty vacationers rushed everywhere, pushing and shoving, grabbing every pamphlet and trail map, generally wasting the place.

I herded our group to the back of the center for a quick inspection of the wall-mounted trail map. In this one-million-acre park, I was determined to find a secluded, quiet spot for all of us to relax.

The map revealed a short, level trail that departed from behind the visitor center and went south to a large lake. I pulled Max off the giant taxidermied grizzly bear he was pretending to wrestle and looked around for Joeline. I found her sitting with her leg propped up watching the park overview video.

She grimaced. "My leg is throbbing. I'm going to stay here while you guys go on your hike."

"Are you sure?" I asked. "We can find something else to do." Truth be told, I would have been okay with that. My own leg wasn't bothering me too much, but I still had pain shooting through my lower back.

"No, you guys go. I like watching these videos. And Angela's staying with me."

I didn't move. It seemed like all I was doing was leaving Joeline behind.

"Go, Marty. Really, I'm good. Go throw some rocks in the lake."

Feeling a pang of guilt, I gathered the older girls and Max, and we departed the center and rounded the corner to the back of the building. Not five minutes into our hike, a bighorn sheep ran past us on the trail. His large, curled horns must have weighed fifteen pounds each. I envisioned a thirty-pound hat on my head. Simply doing that gave me a crick in the neck.

After about a quarter mile, I stopped to take a photo of the kids when five young guys returning from their hike came toward us.

"Do you want me to take a picture of all of you?" the one wearing a Dartmouth sweatshirt asked.

"Oh that would be cool. Yeah," Grace said, twirling her ponytail.

We scrunched together while Grace stood in front of us beaming and posing like she'd just landed on the cover of *Seventeen* magazine. The photographer moved along and most certainly forgot about his kind gesture within seconds. Not Grace.

"Those guys were so hot," she said. "I think the one in the Dartmouth sweatshirt liked me. He was definitely looking at me."

"Of course he was," Mollie said. "You have to look at someone when you're taking their picture. And besides, you were blocking out the rest of us."

"I wonder if we'll see them again. Oh! Maybe they're staying at our campground!"

"I doubt it," Julie said. "You'll have to get into Dartmouth if you want to see him again. Good luck with that." She paused. "Maybe I will see him again."

They both laughed. It wasn't a secret that Julie was the valedictorian of the family.

I continued listening to their boy banter until we stumbled unexpectedly across a ranger blocking the trail, his arms folded across his chest.

"Trail's closed. You'll need to head back up."

"What seems to be the problem?" I asked, annoyed that we had hiked this far, only to be redirected.

"Two bears were sighted at the lake this morning."

"Black bears?"

"Grizzlies."

My blood ran cold. I laughed nervously. "Why don't you just shoo them away?"

Obviously, you don't shoo grizzlies. An image flashed in my mind of Dr. Lane wearing latex gloves and a surgical mask bent over a mauled father and son in a sterile operating room. I stood on my toes and leaned from side to side, looking down the trail, afraid the bears had tired of the lake and were making tracks our way.

The ranger never cracked a smile. He stared ahead stone-faced, his eyes focused on some distant point down the path. "The bears live here, sir. This is their natural habitat. You are just vacationing."

That was my point exactly. The bears could enjoy the lake 365 days a year, whereas my family could enjoy it only one day a year, that day—right then.

"It's not really in a bear's nature to attack humans, but believe me, you don't want your life cut short by a grizzly."

The ranger now had a captive audience of one. Grace and Julie had made an immediate about-face when they were told "you need to head back up"—this was their opportunity to try to catch up to the Dartmouth photographer. Mollie immediately followed, wanting to be included with her older sisters. And Max followed along blindly.

The ranger turned his head toward me without taking his eyes off the trail. "Have you heard of *Night of the Grizzlies*?"

"No." And I was pretty damn sure I didn't want to.

"It's a book by a guy named Jack Olsen."

"Oh. Fiction?"

He snorted. "It's based on a true story, and it happened right here in Glacier National Park."

Oh God, he was going to tell me. I would never fall asleep tonight in a tent.

"One night two girls were attacked by two different grizzly bears. There hadn't been a single fatal bear attack in the fifty-seven years since the park opened. And then two attacks in one night and they were only eight miles apart and happened within four hours of each other."

"Wait a minute. I did hear about this. Both of the girls were eaten, weren't they?"

"Yes, sir." He looked at me for the first time. "That's why the trail's closed."

"I didn't realize that happened at Glacier."

"Sure did."

I started backing up, eager to get out of there before he could give me the grisly details. With a distinct tremor in my voice, I said, "Glad you turned us around. Be careful out here!"

As I hiked back to the visitor center, I kept glancing over my shoulder to check for any bear activity and made a mental note to leave *Night of the Grizzlies* off my summer reading list.

I joined my girls in pursuit of the Dartmouth boys. Why in the hell hadn't they told us the trail was closed? They could have spared me the torment of hearing about another bear attack.

Everyone met up outside the visitor center. After pondering our limited options, I announced that we'd continue driving up the road to see where it took us. All eyes were gazing out the windows when we passed another National Park Service sign directing us up Going-to-the-Sun Road.

"What the heck kind of name is Going-to-the-Sun anyway?" Mollie asked.

Joeline looked over her shoulder. "According to the park video, which I watched on an endless loop, Going-to-the-Sun Road was named after Going-to-the-Sun Mountain."

"And no one knows for sure how the mountain got its name or exactly what the correct name is," Julie said. "The Blackfeet Indians call it The-Face-of-Sour-Spirit-Who-Went-Back-to-the-Sun-After-His-Work-Was-Done Mountain."

"Try fitting that on a street sign," I said.

"Julie, how could you possibly know that?" Grace asked.

"I read it on a pamphlet at the visitor center. Don't you ever pay attention to anything besides boys?"

"No, not really."

I pulled off at a scenic overlook to take in the tall, snowcapped jagged mountains, brilliant green foliage, and clouds so low you could reach up and poke them. We had the place to ourselves, except for the station wagon full of kids pulling in, followed by a bus stuffed with Japanese tourists, and finally six motorcycles. We sped away before the newcomers spilled out.

The road became very windy, narrow, and so close to the edge that you could hear the loose gravel spilling over down the cliff. I could stick my head out the window and see my shadow on the switchback below. My heart was pumping with adrenaline, but when I glanced over at Joeline, she had her good hand braced against the dashboard for impact and her good leg planted firmly on the floorboard.

"Are you okay?" I asked.

"No! While you guys were out hiking, some ranger was telling me all about a family that drove off the road a few days ago."

"I am going pretty slow."

"Martin, they all died. And it was on this road—that we're driving on right now!"

Just then, in a bit of unfortunate timing, we drove past a guardrail that showed signs of recent repair. Directly below it was a flattened swath of foliage, about the width of a car, that stretched about fifty feet down below the cliff.

"For God's sake, Martin, go slower!"

"Honey, if I was going any slower, we'd be backing up."

I was driving ten miles below the posted park speed limit and could no longer see the end of the line of cars piling up behind us. I could, however, clearly see the driver directly behind me, because his face was plastered on our rear window.

Fear is a funny thing—a double-edged sword. Its evolutionary purpose is to keep you from doing things that might kill you. But fear can also drive you to do things that might actually *get* you killed.

In 1978, six of my IBM colleagues and I began laying out plans to scale Mount Whitney in California—the third mountain climbing trip for our group. The fame and pageantry of our travels had been exaggerated wildly to anyone around who would listen.

One unsuspecting victim of our tall tales was a coworker named Ken. He was actually more than a coworker. He was a senior member of the technical staff in our office—an experienced statesman and leader who had served as a mentor to me and others on many occasions. For the previous two years, we had subjected Ken to the aggrandizement of our expeditions at the bar after work. But only a tiny portion of what he had heard was based on facts.

Ken pleaded with us to go on our next adventure, promising he wouldn't be a burden, insisting he could keep up. The guys and I joked with him about accompanying us, never thinking he would actually follow through. One thing was true about the trips—they were grueling. And Ken was not a grueling kind of a guy.

As the time grew closer for our departure, we bought our plane tickets, booked a rental van, and confirmed hotel reservations. We got our gear out and cashed in our paychecks.

Meanwhile Ken employed a clever strategy for joining the team— he pretended we had agreed for him to come along since the start. But while he was planning to go, he was only pretending to get in shape, despite our relentless prodding. We told Ken repeatedly that if he really intended to go, he needed to get in shape to be able to climb the tallest mountain in the continental United States. Do some day hikes. Work out. Carry a loaded backpack around for hours on end.

But he didn't. And because no one had the *cojones* to tell him no, he simply showed up at the airport.

When the seven of us arrived at the trailhead to this 14,500-foot monster, we were outfitted for whatever extreme conditions might confront us on our three-day expedition. We were all set to embark on our ultimate adventure to date when a ranger approached us.

"Say, fellas, be careful. Don't make the same mistake those boys made a couple of days ago. Another ranger and I had to search out their frozen bodies and carry them off the mountain. Late summer snows can kill you. People just don't expect it."

We'd already heard the story. The boys who died had worn shorts, tank tops, gym shoes, and no socks. They had only one sleeping bag and took very little along with them to eat or drink. Unencumbered by any substantial gear, they made excellent time ascending the mountain.

Unfortunately, they were so far up the mountain when the heavy July snowstorm hit, they couldn't begin to get back down through the two feet of crippling snow that quickly covered the trail. They eventually abandoned the effort to descend and huddled together in the one sleeping bag beneath some boulders. That's where the search party found their bodies a couple of days later.

It was a story we were determined not to repeat. We all had significant hiking experience, aside from Ken, a healthy respect for the power of nature, and enough equipment for a two-week expedition in the Himalayas. We thanked the ranger for his advice, comfortable that his concern really didn't apply to us.

The first day of these trips is the investment day—it's all work and no play. Carrying all that weight for such a distance just isn't much fun. The scenery is overwhelmingly magnificent, but our heads usually hung so low that all we could see was our feet trudging forward.

The fun begins on day two. You leave base camp and all your heavy equipment behind, climb easily to the summit (nothing is actually done easily at fourteen thousand feet), cavort for an hour or so, and return to base camp for dinner and celebratory drinks. Airplane liquor bottles serve this purpose very well. The labors of the first day are endured only for the glories of the following days.

We spent the next ten hours carrying hundreds of pounds of gear several thousand feet of elevation and eight miles of distance up the rugged Sierra Nevada. To our amazement, Ken hung in there with us. We may have taken an extra break or two, but no one objected to that.

As darkness fell, thick clouds spilled over the tall mountain peaks to the west. Ian, the most experienced of us, picked out a premier spot to pitch base camp, nestled beneath some cliffs, next to a small lake, with a direct view of the ridges leading up to Mount Whitney.

The clouds continued their descent and surrounded us rather quickly, so it was every man for himself to pitch his tent, stow his gear, and prep some grub.

I watched in amazement as Ken assembled his tent. Not only did he have all the right gear, he knew how to use it. We had worried for nothing. Turned out that Ken wasn't the deadweight we all thought he would be.

Most of us were sufficiently set up for the night when a few snowflakes began to drift in. It had been a beautiful day and snow wasn't in the forecast—as far as we knew. But it would make for a pleasant night's sleep.

The guys and I gulped down a few final morsels and retreated to our respective tents. By then, the snow was falling more heavily and covered the ground. I was in my tent rolling out my sleeping bag when I heard what sounded like a wild animal tearing into our site. I bolted upright, almost piercing the top of my tent, thinking we were being attacked by some enraged beast. Then I heard a couple other guys screaming and yelling, seemingly fighting off the wild animal.

I tore out of my tent and leapt into a jujitsu stance, recognizing the potential of being wasted immediately by this unidentified creature. But in the thickening dusk, all I could see were my companions gathered in something of a semicircle around Ken's half pitched tent—there were some hands waving and some tongues wagging—a confusing scene.

Could it be that the enraged beast was Ken? He was frantically tearing down his tent, stuffing gear into his pack, running around shrieking, "You heard what the ranger said! We're going to die. It's snowing. We gotta get outta here right now or we're going to freeze to death just like those other guys!"

I heard Ian say, "Ken, calm down. Leave your tent up. We're not going to freeze to death. We've got all the necessary supplies. We've got sleeping bags and warm clothes. Everything's waterproof. The snow's not going to get into your tent. We're not in any danger."

"Doesn't matter. Those guys froze to death!"

"Look. We've camped in way worse snow than this. Everything is fine. You need to calm down."

"You guys are crazy! You can stay here and die if you want. I'm going down."

"No," Ian said. "Going down is what will kill you."

But Ken continued packing, scurrying around trying to convince us all we were going to die. He kept muttering to himself. "The ranger said we were going to freeze . . . We should've listened to him . . . Why aren't you guys packing?"

The ranger's warning must have been ticking away in poor Ken's subconscious mind all day long, and when the flakes started falling, he exploded into a conscious level of terror that sent him off the edge.

"This is insane," Ian said to the rest of us. "We spent hundreds of dollars and a year of planning, just to what? Turn around when we're almost at the top? To hike back down a mountain at night in a snowstorm after we just set up camp? That's way more dangerous than staying here. I knew we never should have let him come with us."

"Let him go down by himself," someone blurted out.

"We can't do that," Ian said. "If he goes back alone we'll be searching for his dead body tomorrow."

Ken was finished packing and about to start his six, or seven, or who knows how many hours of trekking back down. He wasn't a full-sized mountain man, but he was too big for any of us to effectively restrain without potentially causing someone a lot of bodily damage. A stable individual would have trouble making the journey alone, much less a frantic one.

So it was decided. We were all going back.

Two of the guys were able to detain Ken just long enough for the rest of us to finish breaking down the campsite. It was with heavy hearts, and packs, that we turned our backs on Mount Whitney.

We were already spent from the ten-hour hike up the mountain. It was well below freezing and the snow was now falling heavily, at least six inches buried the trail. We were crossing over streams, swollen from the snow, on rocks that were coated and slippery, picking our way across slick logs perched high above frosty brooks with forty pounds of gear on our backs.

The blanket of snow gave off just enough ambient light for us to shuffle our way along. Many places on the trail were extremely narrow, and the drop-offs to the side were significant.

Ken trudged down in a zombie-like trance, not saying a word.

Hiking in a snowstorm, in the dark, down a narrow mountain path with a crazed man, rates as an all-time low for me. Waking up at the bottom of the mountain to a gorgeous, cloudless, pristine day—what would have been our summit day—made it even lower.

I never went back to Mount Whitney, and Ken never joined us on another expedition.

Continuing our crawl up Going-to-the-Sun Road, we eventually reached the western glacier valleys. We drove past a section of river where playful vacationers were jumping off some low cliffs into the water. The kids pleaded with me to stop, knowing how easily I would cave. I needed a break from riding the brakes and quickly complied. Joeline elected to remain in the van, and Angela volunteered to keep her company. The rest of us dug through our day bags, found our swimsuits, and raced to the river.

The stream was crystal clear—perfect for cliff jumping. The girls screamed wildly all the way down before the ice-cold water silenced them. They surfaced, laughing and giggling so hard it sounded like they were choking. Max sat next to me squirming. I made him watch his sisters several times to learn the appropriate places for climbing and jumping.

I finally took the strap off his wrist and held my breath as he scampered like a chipmunk up the cliff. He danced around at the top, peering over the edge, and then walked backward, tripping and running into his sisters. God, he was going to kill himself before he even jumped. I was about to scale the rocks and reattach the strap when Max went soaring off and into the water. He popped up like a cork and swam quickly back to shore to do it all over again.

The kids kept jumping until they were shivering so violently they could no longer climb the rocks to the cliff. I blasted the heat on the drive back to the campground. Their teeth chattered nonstop while my brow started beading.

As I circled slowly to our site, a pack of kids darted out in front of the van, and I nearly flattened them. A spry, old woman followed close behind, screaming after them and directing obscenities at me for going too fast. How could the old biddy think I was driving too fast? I barely had enough forward momentum to roll over the speed bumps.

Joeline wanted to attend the campfire program that evening, so we all headed to the small amphitheater. A tall, pale ranger stood on stage, a large yellow-eyed owl attached to his forearm. The ranger discussed some of the predatory wildlife in the park—namely, bears, mountain lions, and the northern hawk owl. I almost raised my hand to tell him about one he was omitting, but she was standing a couple of rows over, giving me the side eye.

After the ranger talk, I was hanging our wet towels and bathing suits on the clothesline when the old lady strolled up.

"I wanted to apologize for my little outburst earlier," she said. "Those darn kids run out into the street without even looking, and it just scares me."

"Not a problem," I lied in return. "I appreciate you stopping by," I lied again. I hung another towel. Why was she still here?

"I'm a physical therapist. I specialize in ambulatory recovery. My name is Ruth."

Ah, that was why. God sent us another angel, and I was being a total jerk. *Get your act together, man—who knows how many other plainclothes angels are wandering about.*

Ruth watched Joeline hobble around the campsite. "You know, if you'd like, I can give you some tips on how to use that cane. I don't know what you were told, but you're not using it quite right."

"No one told me anything," Joeline said.

"Ah, that explains it. Here, let me show you."

She provided a crash course, or rather, a "non-crash" course on proper cane usage. Once Joeline got the hang of it, Ruth said, "If you don't mind me asking, what happened?"

Joeline shot me the "help" look. She wasn't ready to talk about the accident—she might never be. I wasn't all that eager myself, but I jumped in and gave Ruth the two-minute version.

She shook her head. "You know, we're renowned for our parks in

Canada. This kind of thing shouldn't happen there. I have a lawyer friend up in Calgary. Give him a call."

"What for?" I asked.

"Maybe he can help get you some compensation."

It had never crossed my mind to consider legal action, but I took down the number to be polite and we said our good nights.

The kids were in Big Blue. They had turned off their flashlights and were telling ghost stories, terrifying one another. I didn't need to hear a ghost story to be terrified. I couldn't stop thinking about the two deadly bear attacks that happened in this very park, even if it was many years ago.

We were all going to be snuggling up tight, afraid of what was lurking in the dark woods.

20.

a grizzly birthday

Me with Joeline's cane on the afternoon of my forty-fourth birthday,
Glacier Park, Montana.

Wednesday, August 10, my forty-fourth birthday. Camping on my birthday had become a tradition. It started about five years before when Joeline surprised me with colorful crepe paper and festive balloons strung up around our campsite in the Blue Ridge Mountains. She had even brought homemade cherry pies for dessert. We had not been introduced to saskatoons yet.

This year my family started the celebration with an old-fashioned photo shoot. Joeline dressed me up in my old flannel shirt, tattered ankle-length pants, a dusty cowboy hat, and my only pair of shoes, by now authentically weathered and worn.

She wanted an Ansel Adams look, so she borrowed Max's camera, already loaded with cheaper black-and-white film based on our assumption that his entire roll would consist of only rocks and the ground. Joeline snapped several staged photos of the family sitting around the campfire pit. (The kids had a lot more fun posing for the pictures than looking at them later, since the final photos bore little resemblance to anything spectacular that Ansel would have produced.)

Ruth wandered by and warned me that the statute of limitations might be shorter in Canada than in the States. "You need to contact my friend to get something on the books. Quickly."

This wasn't a course of action I would normally pursue, but just in case the Canadian medical bills grew exponentially, I figured a call wouldn't hurt. "Will do."

The girls asked me if they could do a little birthday shopping before we headed off on the hike we had planned. Since their intentions were so noble, I could hardly find it in my heart to deny their request. I drenched out the fire while Joeline corralled the kids into the van, and we drove down to East Glacier Park Village, where I could also try to reach Ruth's friend.

Joeline was feeling more comfortable with her cane now that she was using it correctly. She and the kids left to browse through the mountain boutiques while I went off in search of a pay phone.

There was a booth right around the first corner. My lucky day. Using my MCI card, I dialed several times, but all I heard were high-pitched beeps and piercing squeals. I'd had no trouble when I called Seth, though we were in Canada then. Maybe I should have read the directions on the back.

That helped. I was finally able to connect to an operator who would stay on the line long enough for me to explain that I was in Glacier Park, Montana, trying to place a call to Calgary, Alberta.

"You can't make calls with that card when you're outside the US," she said.

"But I'm not outside the US. I'm in Montana." No response. "Isn't Montana still part of the United States?"

"Yes, it is." She giggled. "But not where you are."

"But isn't *all* of Montana in the United States?" We'd been out of the country for several days, but I wasn't aware of any international border changes. "I'm trying to call from inside the US to outside the US."

"Where you are is considered part of the Canadian system because it's so remote. That's why you can't call from there." She paused. "But I'm not sure why you can't call from outside the States back into the States. Although I must admit I've never heard of that state."

"What state?"

"Alberta," she snapped back.

"That's because Alberta's not a state. It's a province. Provinces are like states, except that they're in Canada."

"Well, sir, now that you understand your mistake, why don't you just dial the number yourself."

"No!" Then it struck me how useless this call had been, and I reconsidered. "That's a splendid idea." Click.

I pulled out my trusty IBM-issued American Express card and was about to dial zero then stopped. I really wasn't supposed to use it for personal expenses. But it shouldn't be a problem—I'd reimburse them. I got an operator right away, gave her the card number, and just like that, she put me through to Calgary.

"Good morning, Barry and Burn's Funeral Home and Crematorium. How can I help you?"

"Uh, this isn't Mr. Chase's law office?"

"No."

"Do you happen to know the number for Mr. Chase's law office?" A ridiculous question, but I had to try.

"No, sir. Never heard of him. Sorry."

"Thanks." I let out a snicker that was a poor disguise for weeping.

Why I persisted I don't know. I suppose it had become something of a crusade for me. I was going to get through to the law firm if it killed me.

I dialed zero again, and the operator put me through to some Canadian directory assistance line. The guy quite cordially provided me with the correct number to the law firm. It was one digit off from what Ruth had dictated to me—or what I had written down. The line rang. I could hardly stand the anticipation.

Someone answered, "Good morning. This is Debbie."

I almost dropped the phone. "Uh, um, hi," I stuttered, now suddenly unaware of what to say. It had never occurred to me that I would actually get through to someone. "Uh, yeah. Is, uh, is Mr. Chase available?" I managed to fumble out.

"Oh, I'm sorry, sir"—the standard response when speaking to me these days—"Mr. Chase is out of the office today." Of course he was. Why did I even ask? "But I'll be happy to review your situation and relate all the details to him."

"Splendid." I gave her a five-minute overview of the incident.

She had just started to explain how their process worked when an eighteen-wheeler pulled up about eighteen feet from my phone booth. The driver, who bore a striking resemblance to John Candy stopped the rig, left it running, jumped out of the cab, and disappeared. His diesel engine could have drowned out a 747 at takeoff.

"Debbie!" I yelled into the phone. "Hold on, there's a tractor trailer next to me. I can't hear a word you're saying!"

It wasn't just that I couldn't hear anything, but more that my head was about to combust—the phone booth had become a giant reverberation chamber. I could hardly hang on to the phone, much less communicate through it.

This went on for several minutes. Where the hell was John Candy?

I wanted to hop in the damn rig and drive it off a cliff. Luckily I had no idea how.

"Debbie," I whimpered, as my forehead slid down the glass enclosure. "Oh, Debbie."

I held up the phone in front of my face and placed it lightly back in its cradle. Debbie was surely long gone by now.

As I was consoling myself with the fact that I'd had no burning desire to call a lawyer in the first place, I saw the kids spilling out of the stores. Their shopping bags indicated that they had been successful in their pursuits. At least someone had.

Our next destination was the Many Glacier area. With its massive mountains, sparkling lakes, and active glaciers, it was the very heart of the park. I asked the ranger at the entrance booth for a recommendation on hikes.

"Well," he said, a smile growing on his face, "one of my favorite places in the whole park is Iceberg Lake."

He stooped a little and peeked inside our van. His bright smile waned. "But it's a haul gettin' up there. And from the looks of your group—"

He was cut short by an upheaval from the back seat.

"We can do it, Dad!"

"Yay, let's go!"

"Come on. We've hiked way farther than that."

"Way farther than what?" I asked. "The ranger hasn't even told us how far it is yet."

"It's just over nine miles round trip, and the trail rises about fifteen hundred feet."

That meant nothing to our crew, but it was a whole lot of "up," combined with a whole lot of "over."

The juvenile insurrection continued. "Dad, we'll be fine."

Even Joeline voiced her consent. "Give it a try. If it's too much, just turn around. Angela can stay and keep me company."

And that was that.

We made our way to the parking lot at the Swiftcurrent Motor Inn, the overflow lot for the Iceberg Lake trailhead, where we packed up our lunch and strapped on our hiking gear. Joeline and Angela strolled down the trail with us a short way.

"Can you be back in four hours or so?" Joeline asked before turning around.

That would be cutting it pretty close.

"Sounds reasonable," I said. "Don't worry if it's a bit after that. The hike is fairly long. But we'll do our best."

The trail offered glimpses of the surrounding mountains before sending us into a dense pine forest. We were accompanied by the usual suspects—squirrels and chipmunks—scurrying and pecking away alongside us.

The girls engaged in an interesting social experiment, led by Grace, to no surprise. They picked small samples of wildflowers and then offered their bouquets to the different gentlemen they passed.

These advances were met with a wide variety of responses. Most fellows just took the flowers and smiled without saying anything and continued on. A couple of sour guys abruptly refused the offering, admonishing the girls for blatantly defacing the park.

And then there was the young Frenchman, in his camouflage beret, who magnanimously kissed the little coquettes' hands in a chivalrous display of appreciation. "Ah, *merci, merci! Belle!*" The girls' faces flushed red. The man was doing some beaming of his own. I finally had to prod him, ever so politely, on his way. Max imitated him, flitting between his sisters, grabbing their hands, and trying to kiss them before they could yank them away.

I had to interrupt the silliness. "Time to close down the floral shop, ladies, and focus on the journey. Let the flowers grow where God planted them."

Turns out I was raising little mountaineers. I was a proud dad when we arrived at Iceberg Lake in just over two hours. It was stunning—and appropriately named. The cerulean-blue water was dotted with blindingly white, large chunks of ice floating around at the whim of the winds blowing down the cliffs.

The shoreline was strewn with large, smooth rocks, the perfect size for young children to sit on while wolfing down their lunch. Chomping on some trail mix, Mollie pointed. "Look at all those giant icebergs."

"You don't see those in the Smokies," Julie said.

"Can we climb onto one of 'em, Dad?" Max asked.

"Max, little dude, that water is so freezing cold it would burn your feet right off."

"Dad, that doesn't make any sense. Water doesn't burn you."

"When it's that cold, it does."

The kids chose to learn the hard way. All eyes followed Grace as she took off her shoes and socks and then stepped off a rock into a foot of ice water.

She instantly took on the appearance of a cartoon character with its finger stuck in a light socket—rigid and electrified, eyes and mouth wide open, unable to breathe.

It took about two seconds for her to return to life. She came tearing out of the glacial water, skinning her shins on the rocks along the way. I had no more arguments about berg-surfing.

Max and the girls threw a couple of hundred rocks into the lake. Their cheering echoed off the canyon walls whenever they succeeded in landing a projectile on a berg. I gazed overhead as several mammoth birds of prey floated effortlessly between the massive cliffs draped with hanging glaciers, each emitting a glistening streamlet down into the emerald lake shimmering before us.

I could have stayed in that paradise forever.

But the sun was sinking lower in the sky, so depart we must. We had no chance of making Joeline's four-hour request if we didn't move it along. She would worry about us regardless of how long we were gone, but if we missed curfew, her mind would go into overdrive picturing worst-case scenarios.

The trail back was strangely devoid of fellow hikers. Although I appreciated the solitude, there was comfort in numbers—the presence of additional hikers always helped deter bears from loitering about. My stomach tightened as I began to picture my own worst-case scenario.

Rounding a tight bend into a steep descent, we were once again surrounded by a profusion of wildflowers. Wait a minute. Hadn't the rangers told us that bears like to snack on flowers? Was this velvety violet stuff a delicacy of choice? It was early evening, aka feeding time. I urged the girls and Max to pick up the pace.

The vast majority of bear attacks occur on solo hikers, rarely on larger groups of like six or more. Now, of course, there were only five of us, but I was confident we could make the noise of six, or even eight, because we usually did and had done so most of the day.

But my exhausted little group was proceeding along like a quiet funeral procession. They had nothing left after covering well over a thousand feet of elevation in seven miles. It was time for a very pointed reminder about the benefits of bear avoidance. "Hey, kids, you don't want to get eaten by a bear, do you?"

That's all it took. Grace yelled "Hiiiii Yogiiiii" followed by Julie's scream "Heyyyy Smokeyyyy" as we marched down the trail. I joined in hollering, "What was I thinkinggg ?" We made enough noise to frighten away a T. rex. No self-respecting, peace-loving bear would consider approaching such a raucous hoard of hikers.

As we continued down the slope, the sun descended behind the mountain and a cool breeze rustled the leaves around us. Our declining trajectory led us past a large huckleberry patch. I'd thus far resisted the temptation to sample any wild fruit, but since we were pretty far along, one quick berry wouldn't slow us down.

I searched out one plump, ripe berry, snatched it off its branch, and examined it closely before popping it into my mouth. Delicious. I looked around for one more sample. A tart salmonberry, easy to identify by its distinctive color, many of which were flourishing alongside the huckleberries.

About a mile from the trailhead, we came upon two rangers sitting on the high side of the trail a short distance in front of us. Had they seen me eat those berries? Surely, they weren't going to give me grief for eating two tiny little berries. I began hurriedly wiping my mouth on my sleeve. The rangers kept looking straight ahead.

"Keep moving, folks," one of them said in a calm, hushed tone. "There's a bear just off the trail."

"Black bear?" I asked.

"Grizzly."

No kidding. Jack Olsen was about to get his sequel: *Evening of the Grizzlies.*

I looked out of the corner of my eyes without moving my head. Directly below us, about twenty feet off, I spotted the tell-tale hump of an enormous grizzly bear. He was marauding about on all fours, grazing profusely on aster, huckleberries, and wild salmonberries—pretty much exactly what I had just taste-tested.

He raised his immense head and then stood up on his hind legs. Holy crap, he was monstrous. As he loomed higher over the meadow, the mountains shriveled and shrank behind him. His menacing eyes bore a bite-sized hole right through me. He let out a deep grunt, giving us a glimpse of his razor-sharp canines. Then he dropped to all fours and burrowed back down into his bushes, leaving only the curve of his hump to intimidate us.

A primal impulse surged through my body—protect my offspring at all costs. I flashed back to Ken's behavior on Mount Whitney. *Keep your wits about you. Don't get irrational.*

I whispered to my kids, "Keep moving forward and keep talking. Don't look at the bear." Telling a kid not to look at a bear is like telling them not to eat an ice cream cone they had just licked. But I'd read somewhere that a grizzly interprets eye contact as a sign of aggression.

The girls did their best to look ahead while trying to surreptitiously sneak glances. Max didn't bother sneaking—he openly stared at the grizzly. "I'm gonna wrestle with it!" he said, slipping off the trail, his hands outstretched. The rangers shot up. I swooped in like a hawk on prey, silent and on point. I had a death grip on my son. Why hadn't I put the safety strap on him? The bear let out a warning growl from the bushes.

No one was talking now. We tiptoed past the grizzly in complete silence, Max squirming in my arms. Despite my instructions to keep chatting, we were all too frightened to make even a peep.

Luckily the bear had returned to his smorgasbord of berries. We maintained a brisk pace down the path. About thirty feet past the bear, I paused for a second to set Max down, still keeping an extremely tight grip on his hand. When I turned to check on the grizzly, he was now moving up the hill. Was he circling around behind us?

We were being stalked! *Quit looking, you idiot—keep walking!*

I glared up toward the rangers, who were now just above us, assuming they would be swinging into action, but they just sat there talking quietly to each other. They seemed content to relax and watch the bear bear down on us.

"Don't worry," one of the rangers said. "He's just meandering up the hillside. You're fine. But you do need to keep moving."

How would you not worry when a grizzly was tracking you?

For the first time I noticed small rifles lying across the rangers' laps. We hurried along as fast as we could without breaking into a run. My heartbeat slowed the farther down the trail we went. Maybe the presence of the rangers keeping watch gave me a false sense of security. Maybe the presence of their rifles gave me a true sense of security.

(I later learned that they were loaded with tranquilizers, not lead. I'm glad I didn't know that at the time. It would have taken several rounds of sedatives to slow down that enormous beast.)

The rangers no doubt had closed the trail as soon as they heard about the grizzly bear. This explained the lack of hikers. Joeline would have asked why they closed the trail, and she was probably having a panic attack. Especially now that more than four hours had passed.

The last quarter mile of trail cut through an open field of long, wavy grass. And when the tall gateway we had entered through came into sight, we all ran the final hundred yards.

"I see them, Mommy!" I heard Angela call out.

Joeline hobbled over to the trailhead eager and reached out to hug and kiss everyone, her body shaking with worry and relief. I was relieved that she didn't slug me with her cane.

The kids all chattered excitedly, boldly reconstructing our bear episode, already embellished with creative magnifications. Joeline finally interrupted me. "I have been worried out of my mind about you." Her eyes filled with tears.

I gave her a big hug. "I'm so sorry we're late. I never dreamed we'd run across a bear."

Wiping away her tears, she said, "I want you to meet Gloria. We've been waiting together for you guys and her husband." She swung her arm around to introduce her, but found herself waving at an empty field.

Joeline did a double-take. "Oh. That's weird. She was right here. She must have gone back to the inn."

I put Angela on my shoulders, and we followed the kids back to the parking lot. "Did you at least manage to enjoy part of the day before you found out about the bear?"

"It was nice enough. We mostly hung out at the inn and had some lunch out on the porch. But as soon as I saw the Closed sign, I knew something was wrong. When the ranger told me a grizzly bear was wandering around, I said I was going up there after you, but he wouldn't let me. It's not like I could have gotten very far anyway." She pointed to her bum leg with her cane.

"Then Gloria came along." Joeline looked around for her new, lost friend. "She joked that she'd distract the ranger so I could slip past. She didn't seem worried at all."

At the inn, we conducted a five-minute search for Gloria—to no avail.

"That's so strange. She was right there next to me." Joeline looked around again. "You know what else is strange? Gloria never told me her husband's name, or anything else really. She just kept me distracted while we waited for everyone. I don't know what I would have done if she hadn't come along. I probably would've died worrying about you."

No other hikers had emerged from the trail for Gloria to run off with. In fact, we hadn't seen another person on the trail the whole way down.

We didn't get to meet Gloria, and Joeline never saw her again.

On the road back to the campground, I looked for a place to pick up a birthday pie. I also wanted to check yet again for lantern oil. We'd been back out in the sticks now for a couple of days, and since we had packed four lamps and hauled them across the country, by God, I was going to use them.

We stopped at several curious little places along the way, with no luck on either count. The last place we tried was a grocery store outside Saint Mary. They probably wouldn't have oil in stock, but for sure, they'd carry pie of some sort.

I searched the shelves frantically, but all I could find was an empty space on a shelf labeled "Lamp Oil." And even worse, there wasn't a pie anywhere to be found. Not even a Moon Pie or a tart.

How could a guy have a meaningful party without pie? They had an assortment of cakes. But who ever heard of a birthday cake? That wouldn't do.

I abandoned the quest and slumped over to the cooler to select a birthday beer instead. When I got to the checkout, I asked the clerk, "You wouldn't have lamp oil in the back by any chance, would you?"

"No sir. Just sold the last can this afternoon. Been a big run on it, you know."

"No, I didn't know, but I should've guessed."

He then proceeded to ring up $3.75 for my one lousy Bud Light. So I shelved that idea as well. I wouldn't enjoy a Bud Light at $3.75. Maybe a Guinness or Beck's Dark, or something substantial. But not one Bud Light!

Our celebration would have to make it on love and sentiment— and maybe a little duty-free.

After a campfire-cooked meal of hot dogs and sausages, it was time to open the gifts the kids bought that morning. I unwrapped some nice little trinkets, and Joeline had brought some clothes all the way from Charlotte. "Too bad I didn't get you a pair of boots." She laughed.

My family sang "Happy Birthday," their faces barely discernible in the dim glow of the campfire—instead of brightly lit as they would have been if we'd had well-oiled lanterns. Even Joeline sang enthusiastically despite the draining events of the day.

Mere hours before, we had shared a trail with a grizzly. I must be a bear magnet. No one I knew had more bear encounters—besides maybe a park ranger. Come to think of it, it was probably a good thing I hadn't taken that career route.

Bear encounters don't always end with a singalong around the bonfire. This birthday was assuming the status of the best one in forty-four years. True, I had no pie to savor, but every member of my family was alive with their extremities attached.

Tomorrow would be our last day of frivolity, and I was determined to keep everyone safe and in once piece—even if it killed me.

21.

he'll have his on the rocks

Angela, Max, and me getting refreshed in Siyeh Creek, Montana.

Waterfalls have been scientifically proven to reenergize the body. The crashing water generates a bazillion negative oxygen ions that your body absolutely loves. These negative ions are hidden in the spray of the cascading water, so just relaxing by the base of a waterfall and basking in the mist can recharge your internal batteries and has a plethora of positive health effects.

So when Joeline suggested a very short, easy hike to a nearby waterfall, I wholeheartedly agreed. I found two perfect locations on the map where we could get as refreshed as possible on this, our last day in paradise. Surely, no one would get hurt doing that.

Joeline was making steady progress towards normalcy, and though her bandages were about a week old, she'd been able to keep them wrapped and clean. Still, she was eager to have them cut away, or at least changed out and everything cleaned up. She would have to wait only a few more days. We were driving over nine hours back to Seattle the next day and then flying to North Carolina midday Saturday.

On our way up Going-to-the-Sun Road, I pulled into the Saint Mary Lake overlook to shoot some video of the teal-blue water lapping the base of Little Chief Mountain. I was getting some nice footage of the lake and mountain and short clips of the little guys running around at my feet, trying to knock me over.

As I focused in on the crest of the mountain for what was to be the closing shot of the segment, the stench of burning brakes invaded my nostrils—not entirely uncommon in the mountains because of the terrain. But we weren't close enough to any steep grades for the smell to be that overwhelming.

The odor was so pungent the source had to be coming from something nearby, like maybe something I was holding. Just then, the viewfinder went dark. I pulled the $1,500 camcorder away from my face, and a huge plume of thick, noxious white smoke billowed forth from the device.

The recorder died a quick death, taking with it all video evidence of the trip. I had to leave it outside the van for a while to keep from asphyxiating my family.

Farther up the road, we went to the Saint Mary Falls trailhead. It was packed, as you would expect at the entrance to an easy hike. The best parking spot I could get was at the extreme end of the lot, in a spot that wasn't really a spot. I didn't want Joeline to have to start the hike to the falls with a hike to the trailhead. I probably wouldn't have stuck my own vehicle in this distant and exposed location, but that's why you rent a vehicle in the first place.

Just a few hundred feet down the trail, we came upon several wild strawberry patches. Angela was my comrade fruit junkie, so I let her wander through the patch, delicately plucking a berry here and there but mostly just enjoying frolicking in nature's bounty. We slowly fell behind the others, including Joeline. I think it gave her a bit of a morale boost not to be dragging up the rear.

The tranquil hike led to one of the most spectacular falls in the park. Saint Mary Falls drops about thirty-five feet in three separate tiers. The place was invigorating—oozing with negative oxygen ions. We could almost see them floating around.

Julie, Angela, and Joeline were happy to stay there. I went on ahead with Max, Grace, and Mollie to Virginia Falls, said to be equally as impressive. The trail worked its way up the mountainside another two miles, never leaving the side of the stream and its series of smaller cascades. When the falls came into full view, I watched as Max stood stock-still, his mouth falling open, his eyeballs bulging. I had never seen such a sight before. I mean, the falls were really nice, but Max stationary—that was truly amazing.

The stream plummeted about fifty feet straight down along a sheer cliff into a crystal clear, shallow pool. We all took our shoes off and picked our way with some effort to the pool at the base of the falls. The entire area was covered with a micro-thin layer of lichen and moss. We couldn't really see it, but we could feel it on our bare feet as we walked on the wet rocks and in the shallow water.

A large tree had recently fallen across the stream. The ecological hiker would admire this felled log as testimony to the natural cycle of forest life. An adventurous one would admire his or her balancing skills high above the frigid waterfall runoff.

I climbed up onto the log and, with arms outstretched, began wobbling my way slowly across. When my attendant offspring looked up to see me navigating the tree trunk, I feigned imbalance.

"It's pretty treacherous up here!" I shouted. "Stay put and get ready to fish me out if I take a dive."

Their eyes widened like saucers and they obeyed, not their normal response to any of my commands.

"Be careful, Dad!" Mollie said.

I was only a couple of steps out onto the log when I came to a large, vertical limb that arrested my progress. Though not significant in size, this protuberance was perfectly placed and angled to completely stop me.

I was at a standstill, out on a limb, frustrated by this annoying inanimate, small, but complete, obstruction. A feeling of déjà vu washed over me. I'd been in this position before . . . Ah yes, during the Wild West trip.

The five of us were visiting the Colorado National Monument and had hiked about a mile through the desolate and deserted expanse of rocks and cliffs when we came upon a narrow rocky ledge jutting out almost into outer space.

"Marty," Woody said, "Why don't you climb out to the end of that?" He knew I was the most likely to give in to such to an outrageous challenge.

The rest of them joined in, leaving me no alternative but to climb. Oh, the power of a dare, especially a group dare.

The monument is chock-full of pillars, spires, turrets, and rock monoliths as tall as 450 feet, and this ledge appeared every bit that high. To reach it, I had to belly crawl up and over three increasingly large outcroppings of rugged, uneven rocks, sliding over and down the boulder face. The ledge was about four feet wide, with just enough room for me to stand and turn around, spread out my arms, and strike a pose of Hercules.

As the laughter died down and cameras were set to rest, I surveyed the terrain of my return journey.

My original perspective from the mainland—I could probably climb out and back without too much trouble—had now changed. As far as I could tell, there was no way back. I was going to have to live on that ledge forever.

I began tightening up, suddenly very scared.

Although my buddies now seemed miles away, I could hear them clearly. "C'mon, man. You can drag your skinny ass across that turret. You got out there with no problem."

I teetered back and forth for a while and then accepted the fact that if I truly didn't want to live out there forever, I'd have to backtrack. To make matters worse, if that were even possible, it was an incredibly hot day, in the middle of a desert, and I had stripped off my shirt before venturing out. My ascent back up the jagged crests would be costly.

With squeamish determination, I wrapped my naked arms around the scorching promontory and started scrunching my way up like an inchworm, leaving behind a crimson trail of skin.

I didn't dare look down as I clung to the rock and shimmied along for what seemed like an hour. My buddies cheered me on in the distance. I was immortal back then, but immortality would not replace the skin on my chest.

When I skidded down the final rocky knob, I was never so grateful to be back on flat ground.

That night at the campfire, Woody said to me, "I'm so sorry. I never thought for one minute you'd actually go out there."

I wished he had been clearer about that a lot sooner.

Mel, rarely given to personal divulgence, said, "Man, you totally scared the shit out of me. I thought for sure we'd be hauling you outta there with a helicopter."

I looked up at the falls and then down at the water rushing under the log. Having no desire to repeat the monument mishap, I promptly sat down and swung my legs around to reverse direction. I inched my way back to land, aware of my fragile mortality and thankful to be wearing a shirt. I dismounted and moved away from the log and further temptation.

The kids wanted a few more minutes to finish hurling their quota of rocks, after which we returned to Saint Mary Falls. Julie, Angela, and Joeline were fully rejuvenated and ready to move on and get some food. It was midafternoon when we arrived back at the parking lot. We drove a little farther up Going-to-the-Sun Road and pulled over at Siyeh Pass Trail, where we stopped for one last gypsy-style lunch.

A group of travelers frolicked in the brook a couple of hundred feet down the valley. Eager to partake in some frolicking ourselves, we hurried through our meal and headed down to the stream.

Joeline took her time walking down the gently sloping hill and found a level spot to sit and watch her family enjoying the afternoon. She sat down quickly, squatting and balancing with her left hand on the ground, then stretching out her left and then right leg. A slight grimace crossed her face. "It still hurts, but I'm getting the hang of it," she said to me.

"You're doing great. And this is it for the day. We'll leave whenever you'd like."

I walked along the stream a few paces and located an area lined with smooth rocks that slanted downward and ended in a shallow pool.

"All right, guys," I called out, "listen up. If you want to try going down this nice, little slide, sit in the water and scoot your way out to it. But stay off those dark rocks over there because they're slippery."

Grace, Julie, and Mollie waded about in the stream, not interested in getting soaking wet and freezing cold going down the natural slide. Max and Angela, however, were dying for me to give them the all-clear signal.

I did my best to hold their hands as they slid down the rock slide. But doing this task justice would have required the agility of a younger man, optimally one in a wet suit—with footies. After I accompanied them several times through this arctic runoff, the pain signals from my feet were no longer reaching my beleaguered brain.

When I observed that my dogs had ceased barking and had assumed a distinct shade of blue, I tippy-toed back to the bank, sat next to Joeline, and watched our kids having fun on our final day. Everyone twirled and splashed around with big smiles on their faces.

I propped my frosty feet up on a rock, hoping that the last bits of sunshine would thaw them out. The sun sank slowly behind the vast procession of cliffs stretching out to the northwest, casting long, lonely late-afternoon shadows across the canyon. These same harbingers of dusk worked their way up the valleys on the opposite walls of granite. A few light clouds blew around between the peaks, and the calls of distant falcons ushered in the evening coolness. It was that melancholy time of afternoon, when spirits seem suspended between the day's activities and the night's reminiscence. It was the perfect ambiance to mark the end of our vacation.

When my toes started tingling back to life, I stood up to announce that it was time to go. But then I noticed that Max, only fifteen feet away, had ventured out onto the dark rocks, the slippery ones I had specifically told him to avoid. He was hunched over, a little unsteady, glancing down at the rocks and biting down hard on his lower lip. A red flag shot up in my brain like a rocket launch.

I called out, "Max! Don't move. I'll come get you. Stay right there."

He did the opposite, as I should have expected, and began darting back and forth across the rocks, his cold, shivering, skinny little body leapfrogging along the dark, glassy stones.

I lunged forward at a speed previously unknown to me and had advanced to within five feet of him when he bounded onto the last dark, mossy rock. He skidded across the stone, teetered forward, and fell face-first onto a granite slab.

At the moment of impact, there was a distinct single tinging sound, the kind a tiny porcelain object might make if dashed onto a tile floor.

My entire body trembled as he turned his head and peered over at me, his blue eyes wide in shock. I stared back at my son strewn out on the rocks in the river, soaking wet and completely motionless. His mouth hung open, a gaping hole glaring prominently, his two front teeth now lying on the granite slab only inches from a narrow cascade shooting by.

The look on my face must have told him something very bad had happened. He slid his tongue along the stubs, and the poor little guy convulsed, frantically calling out "I want my teeth back" over and over.

By this point, I had bolted the final few feet and grabbed him up out of the water, just in time to hang on to him as he began wailing like a banshee. I rocked him back and forth. For the love of God, this couldn't be happening.

Max and I stood in that stream for what seemed like an eternity. It broke my heart to look at him. All he had left were two pointy stubs of front teeth, one slightly longer than the other. They had been so big and protrusive, waiting patiently for his face to grow up around them. Now they were short, sharp, and shattered.

Max wanted his old teeth back. I wanted them back for him. And they weren't that old, having just recently come in.

The rest of the family stood paralyzed. We needed to do something, but what? First things first, we had to get back to the van. Without instruction, Grace and Mollie rushed ahead. Angela stayed with Joeline as she hobbled up the hill. Julie had dallied for a moment, but then caught up to me while I carried Max. We all moved as quickly as possible in silence, except for Max's wailing.

My mind was in total chaos. Was this an emergency? The closest hospital was probably way back in Calgary, over three hours away. Glacier Park is one of the most remote parks in the entire US. As we approached the top of the trail, I was overcome with uncertainty—and guilt.

My wounded wife, a veritable encyclopedia on medical issues, had little experience with dental emergencies. My stomach was feeling worse by the minute. Max, Julie, and I finally reached the parking area, where Grace and Mollie were pacing around the van. Angela and poor Joeline were struggling to keep up with the entourage. Things were feeling about as lonely as the long, languid mountain shadows right now.

As I plodded toward the van, holding a sobbing Max in my arms, a gentleman suddenly appeared, striding in my direction, his piercing eyes fixed squarely on Max. "Has the little boy hurt his teeth?"

It was more a statement than a question. He had gray hair, but his voice sounded young.

I stared at the man, speechless. Where did he come from? How did he know Max had hurt his teeth? His head was buried in my chest.

Max glanced up at me and then turned to the mystery man and, without saying a word, opened his mouth.

"Oh, my!" the man said. "Those are bad breaks indeed." He looked at me. "I am a dentist, on holiday from Italy. If you will bring the boy to our RV—we're parked near that gray van there—I can examine his teeth more closely."

Of course. My son knocks his teeth out in this desolate, mountainous forest, and I just happen to bump into a dentist. Oh, yeah, and he's parked next to me.

"That would be wonderful. He was playing around in the stream down there and fell on some rocks. I'm Marty, by the way, and this is Max."

"I'm Stefano."

Joeline had caught up by now, and the two of us, in a state of bewilderment, took Max over to Stefano's RV. I asked the girls to wait near our van. Stefano's wife opened the door and welcomed us in. They both inspected Max's teeth.

"My wife, Marie, is a dentist also," Stefano said.

Of course she is.

Stefano inspected the damage. "Hmm. The nerves are exposed in both teeth. It is likely he will lose what is left of them. There is no great emergency to replace them, but the longer they go unprotected, the higher the risk of additional issues, like infection."

I glanced over at my beautiful wife of so many years—for better or for worse. But why did things just keep getting worse? Joeline was wiping her cheeks and blinking her eyes. I had lost count of how many times she had cried on this trip.

"We like to coat teeth with D-Cal in these situations," Stefano said. "Unfortunately, we don't have any with us. I apologize that there's nothing more we can do."

Marie added, "It is okay for your son to eat, but he should avoid food touching the stubs of the teeth as much as possible."

"Will his teeth start hurting later on?" Joeline asked.

"Probably not, actually," Stefano said. "If there is any pain, it should be mild." He nodded. "Good luck to you."

"We can't thank you enough," Joeline said, trying to hold back more tears.

We joined the girls at the van. After I got Max settled in—it was amazing how calm he was—I slid behind the wheel and turned the key. I glanced over and the RV was gone. How could that be? I shifted into reverse and pulled onto the road, looking straight ahead and then into the rearview mirror. Still no RV. I twisted around in my seat to make sure—nothing. A chill ran down my spine.

"Weren't we just in an RV?" I asked Joeline. "I don't see it anywhere."

She shrugged. "They probably pulled out before we did."

"That fast? We would have seen them. Besides, there's nobody in front of us or behind us." I shook my head. "That makes three."

"Three what?"

"Three random encounters with strangers who have mysteriously appeared right when we needed them and then disappeared right after."

She tapped her cane. "Are you counting Ruth at the campground?"

"No. I guess she would make four—except she didn't really disappear. I was counting the couple at Emerald Lake, your friend Gloria, and now these dentists. What are the chances?"

"And Dr. Lane—although technically, she didn't disappear either."

"Same with the Walshes."

The theme song to *The Twilight Zone* started playing in my head.

When we pulled into the campsite, Max shot out of the van and straight for the rocks. Clearly, he wasn't feeling any pain. In fact, unless his mouth was open, which was most of the time, you couldn't tell there was anything wrong with him. He kept jumping off the rocks, slamming headlong into his sisters to knock them over. Joeline tried to entice him to sit by Big Blue to reduce the likelihood of further damage, but she was too tired to enforce her restrictions.

"Do you want to lose what's left of your teeth?" she asked Max.

"What's left of his teeth?" I said. "What's left of his teeth! Oh God! Why didn't we save what was left of his teeth? I saw the chips sitting right there on the rocks. Maybe they could have reattached them or something."

Julie touched my arm, but I shook her off. "Not now, Julie. Maybe his teeth are still there. I could take a flashlight."

She was pulling on my arm now. "Dad!"

"What!" I looked down at her, annoyed. She uncurled her fingers to reveal two tooth chips. "I picked them up before we left."

"Oh, sweetheart."

"Here, give them to me," Joeline said. "We need to preserve them." She poured some milk into a small Ziploc bag and dropped the chips in.

"Oh neat!" Max said, watching his teeth disappear.

Mollie and Grace ran behind our stash of firewood screaming, "Ew, gross."

The wood pile! I'd almost forgotten. No way was I taking all that timber back across the country. I needed to burn every last twig. Those logs had cost me a small fortune in toil and currency, and by God, I was going to get my flames' worth if I had to stay up until dawn to make it happen.

"Stand back, kids! I'm building a bonfire!" I shouted, chucking a half-dozen logs into the firepit.

This declaration drew cheers from the crowd. We spent our last evening burning the remaining marshmallows to a crisp as the kids danced around and laughed. Why couldn't the whole trip have been like this?

After Joeline and the kids disappeared into Big Blue for the night, I stayed at the campfire and piled on the last of the wood. Anger and frustration and disappointment and resentment pounded in my head.

I channeled all of it into those logs and then into the flames, to be dispersed into the air. Sitting on my hard-earned boulder, I put my head in my hands. The crackle of the fire mercifully drowned out my sobs.

As dusk consumed the cloudless sky, the last bits of daylight slowly faded away, grabbing what remained of our vacation and vanishing into the darkness.

22.

sleepless in seattle

The Wild West van's last stand, Sheridan, Wyoming, 1972.

Men have battled the Rocky Mountains for centuries. Our struggles here were truly insignificant compared to what so many others have endured. The Donner Party's tragedy, their horribly bad luck, compounded by a string of disastrous decisions, made our trip seem like the vacation it should have been.

Max knocked over a stack of breakfast provisions from the picnic table, bringing me back to the campsite. He hardly seemed aware of his newfound deformity, and his sisters, quite uncharacteristically, had not been teasing him about it. He had no pain, a small consolation.

Good thing there was so much work to do. Joeline and I couldn't afford to wallow in grief. We needed to break camp for the final time, a major undertaking in itself. Some items would be used again later in the day or that night, while others wouldn't be used again until the next camping trip (presuming there would ever be another one), like Big Blue and the stove. So things had to be packed up and prioritized. Joeline was the taskmaster. The kids ran around like ants, carrying gear twice their weight and loading it into the back of the van.

We were doing our final inspection of the grounds when a familiar-looking RV pulled up at our site. And a familiar voice with an Italian accent called out, "I wanted to stop by and see if the little boy made it through the night okay."

Glacier Park is the size of Rhode Island. How did Stefano find us? We never told him where we were staying.

What more proof did I need that angels lived among us? I was tempted to walk over to him and poke his arm to make sure he was real. But supernatural creatures all seem perfectly real.

"Uh, yes, thanks. Max is doing fine. We're getting ready to scout out some D-Cal right now."

"Best of luck to you all. We've got to hurry on. It was good to see you again."

Before Joeline could even get over and thank them, they had driven away. "That was Stefano? How'd he know we were here?"

"I guess the same way all the other angels knew where we were."

We stood there, our mouths open, as the RV disappeared into the forest.

I drove us up and over Going-to-the-Sun Road one last time. The park was full of sharp, snow-covered peaks fringed and supported by lush, verdant valleys. I could live there if I had to. I'd just need some help providing three squares—and most everything else.

Part of me was happy to be returning to civilization, but a lot of me was dreading the return to normalcy and all the obligations and responsibilities that went with it. One of which had already begun—locating a dentist's office. Our destination was Seattle, but we needed to stop in any town along the way that might harbor a dental practice.

Following the road map to the small town of Libby, Montana, I parked the van at the first dental shingle I came across and stepped inside the office. Before I could say anything, the receptionist said, "Sorry, sir"—where had I heard that before?—"the dentist's not in today."

"Where is the next closest dentist?"

"You can look for one in Troy, just down the road about twenty miles."

We drove on to the even smaller town of Troy, Montana. Or had we crossed into Idaho? I wasn't sure. The little towns all bore a striking resemblance. We might have been in Troy, unless I had accidentally circled back to Libby. In my current mental state, that was a definite possibility.

A sign reading "Troy Hardware" confirmed our location. Seven sets of eyes peered out the windows looking for a DDS sign. Julie spotted one first. I ran in. "Dentist's not in today." I ran back out.

"Dad, I'm starving!" Max shouted as I buckled up, followed by similar complaints from his sisters.

Fine. There was a convenience store adjacent to the dental facility. I grabbed a bag of chocolate-covered doughnuts and a half gallon of chocolate milk—not the healthiest choices, but sometimes in man's quest for tranquility, he must succumb to the will of the masses. We blazed out of Troy in complete silence, the kids descending upon the doughnuts like a pack of wolves on meat.

Glancing down periodically at the map balanced on my thigh, I took us across the border into Idaho. We searched the main drag of Bonner's Ferry and then the side streets. It had become a competition at this point—who could be the first to spot a dentist's office? Joeline won by default in this town, the kids too busy fighting over the chocolate milk. This time, I left the van running.

"Dentist's not in today."

"Okay. So, ma'am, we're kind of having a dental emergency here. Is there any dentist around who can help us?"

"No."

I thought for a moment. I had been living out in the sticks for almost two weeks where the days on the calendar pretty much all blurred together. I used my fingers to do some minor calculations. "Today is Friday?"

"Yes, it is."

"Wouldn't at least one dentist be working somewhere?"

"You're not from around here, are you?"

"No, I'm not. But my son knocked his front teeth out of his head, and he really needs to see a dentist."

"Honey," she said sympathetically, "dentists don't work on Fridays."

At least I finally had an explanation for all the dental vacancies. But now what?

Back in our vehicle, we inched on, ever closer to our final destination, still over five hours away. When we came to Sandpoint, I sped past the dentist's office and drove straight to the hospital. This time I brought Max inside with me. I told him to smile for the receptionist. It turned out that I didn't need to do this, because the staff was extremely nice and helpful, and, most importantly, operating.

Joeline and the rest of the kids wandered in. The nurse confirmed that we would be lucky to find a dentist working anywhere in the state that day, including their little hospital. But they had an intern on hand who could assist. Joeline's eyebrows rose with apprehension.

A young man bounded in to consult with us. After a moment's inspection, he told us he would be back with a tube of D-Cal and we'd be on our way in about fifteen minutes.

"Wow," I said with a sigh of relief. "We just had to find the right place."

The intern returned empty-handed. "Seems we're out of D-Cal." He stared down at his shoes.

I clenched my teeth in frustration—should have known. "Well, where can I get some?" Why hadn't I thought of that before? I'd coat his damn teeth myself. Surely, you didn't need a medical degree to do it.

"You can't. It's a controlled substance. We have to special order it." He took several steps backward. "I'll go do that now."

The nurse escorted us back out to the lobby and told us to have a seat while she made a few calls. But Joeline and I turned toward the door. Why hang around for more bad news?

"Wait! I found a dentist about an hour south of here in Coeur d'Alene. They wouldn't let me schedule an appointment, but when you show up, they said they'd try to work you in."

She gave me directions back to the interstate, and we left feeling cautiously optimistic. Close to four o'clock, the whole family walked into the office of Dr. Lemmons, the fourth dentist of the day, and crowded into the waiting area. The receptionist asked for my insurance card and immediately called the number listed.

"No answer," she said.

I smiled. "Then you've dialed the right number."

Dr. Lemmons finished with his last patient and graciously saw Max. About twenty minutes later, his teeth were cleaned up and coated with D-Cal. Dr. Lemmons advised us not to let Max eat anything for a few hours to allow the coating to dry, but after that, he could eat pretty much whatever he wanted, except for maybe apples and peanut brittle.

We thanked him for working us in and then drove west out of town and directly into Spokane—just in time for rush-hour traffic. It took over an hour to get around the small city. Who knew there could be so much rushing in Spokane?

Several miles outside of town, I glanced in the rearview mirror at Max. He was making funny noises and sloshing with his mouth, moving his jaw around like he was trying to tie a knot in a cherry stem. Considering we had no cherries, it didn't take long for me to guess what he had done.

We had hopscotched our way across Montana and down most of the Idaho panhandle, stopping at every dentist's office in the two states, plus a hospital. My knuckles tightened on the wheel. "Joel, I think Max has licked all the D-Cal off his teeth."

She twisted in her seat and inspected Max's mouth. She shook her head slowly and closed her eyes, confirming my fear.

"What are we supposed to do now?" I asked, choking up.

Joeline reached over and put her hand on my shoulder. "Just keep driving."

I couldn't speak.

"Look, the dentist cleaned Max's teeth up, and I'm sure there's still some D-Cal left on them. We'll be home tomorrow, and at least he's not in pain. There's really nothing else we can do."

I relaxed my grip on the wheel and distracted myself by enjoying the last bits of scenery. Mount Rainier loomed impressively over the entire southern landscape. The waxing crescent moon touched Rainier's shoulder, and the remnants of sunset left an orange halo around the peak. Overhead, the evening sky was an ombré of blue. A stunning scene that helped me escape, if only for a few minutes.

Close to ten that night, I pulled off the interstate and went directly to a Motel 6 we had spotted. We were near North Bend, about thirty miles outside Seattle. With all our driving and stopping, we'd been on the road for over thirteen exhausting hours and covered over five hundred miles. Everyone was in desperate need of some personal space.

But our long day didn't come close to the final leg of the Wild West trip—the granddaddy of all hauls.

After two and a half months of hard vacationing and twelve thousand miles of travel, our old, faithful customized van started showing signs of terminal deterioration. Chugging up the mountain pass leading to Lake Tahoe late one morning, the van began losing power. It crept along, moving slower and slower until it finally sputtered, choked, and rolled to a stop. We were many, many miles from any service station, and God forbid any of us had AAA coverage.

The easiest alternative, and only practical one, was to point the van back down the mountain. This meant four of us had to push the van back and forth to reverse its direction while Couzy, the smallest of the group and the self-professed weakest, manned the wheel.

Once inverted, the van improved significantly, largely due to the laws of gravity. The poor vehicle labored itself into near exhaustion over the next few days, somehow managing to transport us all the way to Sheridan, Wyoming. But the next morning, we spent half an hour getting the old girl started. Walt turned it off later when we stopped to get ice for our cooler, and upon our return, it wouldn't start. We piled out and pushed it to the town mechanic, Couzy at the wheel.

"Looks like you fellas gunna need to replace some valves and lifters, probably need a new carburetor. I can git you a rebuilt one for cheap. Might need a new starter too. I can git you a rebuilt one of those too."

"And, uh, how much are we talking here?" I asked.

"Oh, at least a thousand dollars. Maybe a little more."

If we emptied all our pockets, we couldn't come up with a hundred dollars. I asked him, "Can you just start the van?"

He let out a hearty laugh. "Sure I can. But if I wuz you, I wouldn't never turn it off again till I got to Ohio."

So that was our new plan.

He tinkered around under the hood and got the van started, and we left her running for the next thirty hours—until we returned to Cincinnati, fourteen hundred miles later. When we needed gas, we kept the engine on while we pumped. We took one detour—Mount Rushmore. The presidents watched stone-faced as Mel streaked past their memorial. He reluctantly redressed and stood guard over the ignition while the rest of us paid homage in a more discreet manner.

In general, I would not recommend traveling this way. On second thought, considering the geography between South Dakota and Ohio, it might be the preferred method.

Shortly after turning off the van, Walt was able to sell it at a profit, despite its deteriorated condition.

At the Motel 6, I was far too tired to play the invisible children trick, so I asked about a room, or two, for seven people, whatever. The man behind the desk, whose bright gold name tag read "Stanley" in bold black letters, laughed. "We're booked solid for the next three weeks."

I stood there staring, numb at this point.

"Just about everything's booked in town," he went on. "I can't imagine there's anything left anywhere. It's been like this for the last couple of months. Why didn't you call ahead?"

I asked to borrow his phone. We couldn't drive around all of Seattle aimlessly wandering in and out of every hotel within the city limits in search of a room at this hour. No way would I leave his hotel lobby without getting something booked. This objective came under immediate attack, when over the next ten minutes, at least five cars pulled up to the front doors and someone jumped out, ran in, asked for a room, and ran out again, darting off into the night in search of that elusive last room—to avoid being sleepless in Seattle.

In the meantime, Stanley's wife, Betty, was calling their "network" to inquire about any open rooms. I also called around, but Stanley was right—everything was booked. It was eleven o'clock by now and I was out of ideas. Pacing in front of the front desk, I rubbed my neck and bit my lip. What the hell were we going to do?

Stanley dispatched another somber-looking young couple out into the night. As the front door slammed shut, Betty motioned me over. She hung up the phone and smiled. "That was one of our network motels calling back with a room. Don't ask, just go. They'll hold it as long as they can."

"Oh, thank God! Go where?"

"It's right next to the airport." She roughed out some directions saying "Go, go, go" and chased me out.

The airport? That's perfect! I ran out the door, jumped in the van, handed Joeline the scribbled directions, and took off.

When we reached top speed, I looked over at Joeline. "You don't think Betty was trying to . . . ?"

"Just drive. And pray."

Betty's directions were sketchy and didn't match the roads we were on. We zigzagged through Seattle, half following her directions, half following signs to the airport. Miraculously, we found the hotel. I pulled the van to a screeching halt right outside the entrance and, without turning it off, shot through the hotel doors, gasping out, "Do you still have the room? I just came from the Motel 6, and Betty said you'd hold a room for us."

The elderly woman behind the desk smiled at me and looked down at her keyboard. Did she not hear me or was she enjoying torturing me? She finally received some signal from a gentleman partially concealed away in the back office. Her smile widened even further, and she said most sincerely, "Your room is ready, sir."

I wanted to kiss her, but was afraid that might have been unacceptable. My wife certainly wouldn't have accepted it. I did, however, accept the room.

I parked the van, and everyone gathered the few belongings they had left readily accessible—toothbrushes and clothes to sleep in. The seven of us stuffed ourselves into a room for four. The kids ran around claiming their sleeping spots on the floor, Max closest to the window to watch the planes and the girls cozy in the corners.

Everyone was much too tired to eat dinner. The room came with an all-you-can eat breakfast the kids could hoover up in the morning.

After helping Joeline into bed, I went over to the window next to Max and we watched several planes take off into the night sky. Letting out a huge sigh, I slumped down onto the bed. In a few short hours we, too, would be on one of those planes, heading east.

23.

seven volunteers

One final sweep, Seattle, Washington.

The wake-up call rang like a fire alarm and sent me flying out of bed. I spun my head around trying to figure out where the hell I was. For the last two weeks, the soothing sounds of nature had gently roused me. This manufactured attack on my ears jarred me back to civilization.

We were going home that day, though not before Joeline and I tackled our expedition's final chore: prepping our cargo for the flight. But first things first. We all followed Max's lead in sniffing out the continental breakfast. Joeline and I grabbed a doughnut each and then left for the parking lot.

I pulled the van around to an empty corner, and we set about packing everything into the few boxes and containers that had survived the trip. We weren't going to subject ourselves to the dramatics that always accompanied the loss of items the kids had accumulated, like a favorite rock or some petrified critter. So while they enjoyed endless piles of pastries, Joeline and I sorted, combined, wrapped, discarded, folded, bent, crammed, taped, and tied everything for the long haul across the country.

We had plenty of food left over from the trip, mainly aged cheese, peanut butter, three mostly empty jars of jelly, several crushed cereal boxes (two of which were unopened—not the sugary ones), orange juice, lots of hot dogs (many with bites out of them and most of them burned), two pieces of chicken (not obvious if they had been cooked or not), and a smattering of items that could not be identified. It all had to be eaten, or, more likely, disposed of.

While I swept out sixteen days' worth of debris from the van, Joeline hobbled back inside and pried the kids away from the never-diminishing stacks of food. Several of them managed to assemble to-go plates, squirreling a muffin away in a pocket or a single-serving cereal box, before being dragged away.

We made one stop to fill up with gas, and then I drove to the curb-side check-in at the airport. The kids helped me unload the carry-on bags, two camera bags, airplane games, snacks, and all eighteen pieces of checked luggage.

As I set the last bag down, an attendant approached us. "Sorry, sir, but this counter is closed. If you bring your luggage down to the next door, I can help you."

"You couldn't have told us that five minutes ago?" I asked, peering over the top of my sunglasses.

"I didn't see you until it was too late. No worries."

How could he not have seen us? We looked like a carnival coming to town.

I shrugged. Moving the pile would keep the kids busy while I returned the van. I had called Rent-a-Wreck to tell them I was coming and to get directions to the drop-off location. If the gentleman on the other end of the line had been scouting for Lewis and Clark, they'd still be looking for St. Louis. How would I ever find the place?

After a couple of wild guesses, I ended up heading north on an interstate, but I was pretty sure Rent-a-Wreck was south of the airport. I exited the highway only to merge onto another one going west. At this point I got nervous. I started this jaunt with barely enough time to drop off the van and return to the airport, and I had now wasted almost half of it. Pulling off at the first exit, I was relieved to see signs directing me back to the airport.

This led me straight back to the curbside check-in, where I saw that my family had apparently moved successfully inside. For good measure, I rolled down my window and yelled out to the attendant, "No worries!" At least I knew where I was, even if it wasn't where I wanted to be.

It was entirely possible that I had lost my mind and was now driving in circles around the airport like a hamster on a wheel.

As I exited the airport for a second time, I made sure to turn in the opposite direction than I had gone the first time. With surprising ease and quickness, I accidentally happened onto my destination street, albeit in the wrong direction, "NO U-TURN" signs posted everywhere and a wide median as far as I could see. Several miles and several turns later, I had somehow located the rental car lot, with about thirty minutes until takeoff.

I left the keys in the van and bolted for the courtesy shuttle, begging the driver to speed me to the airport. I raced across the terminal, scrambled through security, and ran down the D concourse like a high school track star, hurdling suitcases and dodging old ladies. I arrived at our gate huffing and puffing, only to find my long-faced children draped listlessly over their chairs.

"Our flight to Charlotte is overbooked," Joeline spat out. "And since we were late, we've been bumped."

Her scowl made it clear we hadn't been "bumped" to first class.

"But that's not possible," I said, trying to catch my breath. "We have confirmed seats. And you have boarding passes, right?" She nodded and gave them to me. "How late can we be? For Christ's sake, people are still boarding the plane!"

"That's what the agent at the gate told me." The devastated look on Joeline's face killed me more than being bumped. "He said we were late, and because of that, they bumped us off the flight. You go talk to him."

I put my hand on my forehead and felt the veins popping out like suitcase handles. You could have picked me up and stowed me in an overhead compartment. I stalked over to the culprit Joeline had pointed out.

I handed him our passes, with the meanest, badass glare I could muster. "I assume we can board the plane now?" I motioned for the kids to head to the gate entrance.

He glanced curiously at my forehead. "No, sir. The Charlotte flight is oversold and you were late."

I am, by nature, more of a negotiator than a fighter, and I resolved to give it one more try. "We have boarding passes for our confirmed seats. However, if the flight is overbooked and you need a few passengers to volunteer to take a later one, we could maybe do that."

This was essentially the airline equivalent of being fired versus accepting an early retirement package. If they bumped us off the flight for being late, that was being fired. There was no compensation. On the other hand, if we volunteered to take a later flight, that was accepting an early retirement package, which (in those days) came with perks: free plane tickets, food vouchers, and, if required, overnight accommodations. Since I was afraid the agent wouldn't budge, we'd be better off accepting a compensation package.

"How many of you are there?" he asked.

"Seven. But my son and wife are both experiencing medical emergencies. They really need to fly out as soon as possible." Maybe my act of generosity would in turn secure seats on this flight for at least Joeline and Max. "But the rest of us can delay as long as you need."

I was now expecting to have the choice of getting on the flight as originally planned or taking the compensation package. This was a sure sign of battle fatigue.

"Okay." He tapped away at his computer. His face scrunched up, and he tapped a little harder. The harder you tap, the faster your computer goes. He frowned and then grimaced and scratched the back of his neck, all the while diligently avoiding any eye contact.

He lowered his face right down to the keyboard and gave one last dramatic stroke before looking up at me. "You can take a seat. I'll let you know."

What? Had we been fired or not? I hated being left in limbo.

Gritting my teeth, I marched back to Joeline.

"You were over there for a while. I guess we're back on the plane?" She glared at me, knowing full well we weren't back on the plane.

"Not exactly." I dropped into the empty seat next to her, scrambling to come up with a positive spin. "You and Max might be, but it's looking like the rest of us might have to take the next flight out."

"What did you do?" she asked, her eyes narrowing. "You were supposed to get *all* of us back on that flight!"

The last few passengers were trickling through the gate. Boarding was almost complete.

"Yeah, I know. But before, we were all definitely bumped off the flight. Now you and Max might get on. Those who don't will get a real nice compensation package. Free tickets and food, and we'll be on the next flight out of here. I know this isn't ideal, but in a few weeks"—I gulped—"or months, we won't remember any of this inconvenience and we'll have free plane tickets! Think of it like being reimbursed for this trip and all the things that went wrong."

Joeline looked at me, shaking with nerves. "Let me get this straight. We don't have any clothes or anything else with us, except for these two lead-weight camera bags. And we're going to spend another day here, with no place to stay and no means of getting around, so we can get free tickets from an airline that's going bankrupt so we can do what? Fly back out here and do the whole thing over? Martin, I'm never going camping again."

So much for my positive spin. She had a good point—several of them. I only had one good point—and she didn't appreciate it.

I huddled up in my seat while she thought about it.

"Well," she said, "I suppose it would be nice to get free plane tickets. Nothing is cheap when you have five kids, especially flying." She wiped away her tears and then leaned in closer to me. "We're taking those free tickets and going to the French Riviera."

That was an idea I could go along with.

The boarding line was now gone. I went back to the counter. Several standby passengers were pacing around, all ready to pounce. The attendants were shuffling paper back and forth wildly, counting tickets, recounting tickets, clicking away anxiously on their keyboards. The main attendant motioned me to approach. "We need seven volunteers. I can confirm your wife and son on the red-eye eleven-thirty flight tonight. The rest of you might get on, but if not, you'll be confirmed on the seven-thirty flight tomorrow morning."

"Red-eye" is airline code for "you adults are going to be awake and squirming in your seat all night long, and your eyes will turn blood red, while your kids get a great night's sleep and will keep you awake for the rest of the day after you land."

"Okay. Great! Let's do it."

The attendant started asking me more questions than my kids did when trying to delay bedtime. He confirmed all the details and then handed me an envelope. "Here are seven round-trip tickets, a certificate you can use at any area Hampton Inn, and vouchers for the airport restaurants."

I had officially retired, and I immediately put that package to good use.

It had been a couple of hours since the buffet line and Max was hungry—and angry. I stopped at the first food stall. They were hawking hot dogs and chips. Max loved hot dogs, except when he was in convulsions. He was going to get one now, even if I had to deposit it directly down his throat. Since he had lost the use of his front teeth, I cut the hot dog into little pieces for him and forced them into his little face. Once this initial charge of hot dog intake started to take effect, he slowly reentered a semi-human state.

Next I called the Hampton, explaining to the clerk that we were traveling on USAir and had volunteered to take a later flight to help out the airline. I laid it on thick, hoping their partnership with the airlines would give us priority status for a room. There was a distinct possibility that Julie, Grace, Mollie, Angela, and I were going to be spending another night in Seattle. My tactic worked. After eating our way through the vouchers, we hopped on the free shuttle to the hotel.

As we entered the Hampton Inn, I noticed a "No Vacancy" sign. I waltzed up to the desk. "Reservation for Ohlhaut."

"Yes, sir," he snapped from behind the desk, and clicked away on his little keyboard. He studied his screen, looking puzzled, and then clicked some more.

"I'm sorry, Mr. Ohlhaut, we don't show any reservations for you here today. Do you have a confirmation number?"

"Yes, I do. Here it is."

He clicked away, then clicked some more, and then harder. Shaking his head, he said, "Sir, it looks like this reservation is for the Bellingham Hampton, about one hundred miles north of here."

I reached out and grabbed the knot of his tie and adjusted it to a neck size of 4½. "Pal, if we're not in the complimentary presidential suite, sipping martinis and relaxing in the hot tub, in less than ten minutes, this tie goes to 2¾. Any questions?"

Okay, I didn't do that, but I enjoyed the brief fantasy. This was clearly their mistake, and I was confident they would straighten it out. Unless, of course, it was my mistake. That was a disturbing thought, and just as the severity was sinking in, he said, "It looks like we're going to be able to get you a room here tonight after all."

It was not the presidential suite. There were no martinis. But I could see Mount Rainier from our window. We all relaxed until eight, when we left the hotel but didn't check out. I had no idea whether any of us would be returning later if we didn't get seats on the plane. We hopped on the shuttle back to the airport with plenty of time to spare.

In fact, arriving at our gate so early made Joeline happy but made me uneasy. I hadn't ever been this timely before. We milled around for over an hour until they announced our flight. Because of their injuries, Max and Joeline qualified for pre-boarding. Walking down the boarding ramp, both of them looked over their shoulders, not knowing if they'd see us on the plane in a little bit or if they'd see us back on the other side of the country. Or given the way things had been going, maybe they'd never see any of us again.

The rest of the confirmed passengers boarded. The flight turned out to be very full, but not overbooked. A flight attendant came out and held a hushed conference with the other attendants, and then called for passengers "Ohlhaut" to come to the desk. "There's an available seat next to your wife. Do you want it?" she asked.

Before I could say yes, Angela ran onto the plane followed closely by an attendant. Shortly thereafter, two more empty seats were found, and Julie and Grace raced to fill those. And amazingly, another spot appeared. Mollie hugged me before departing.

And there I was. Standing all alone—everyone in my family now seated on the plane, except me. As I watched the gate agent close the door to the boarding ramp, I couldn't help but feel a pang of loneliness being left behind.

I took a seat, intending to watch the plane take off before returning to the Hampton. As I stared at the 787, the boarding door reopened. The same attendant emerged, cupped one hand around her lips, and, in a loud whisper, called to me, "There's one seat left! Hurry, hurry!"

As it turned out, a party of well-pickled fishermen, in their attempts to salvage some elbow room for themselves, had loaded their gear into the empty seat between them. When the attendants asked the guys about the seat, they told a tale of holding it for a mythical buddy who had gone to use the lavatory.

Their scam might have succeeded, except that Joeline happened to be seated right in front of them. Overhearing their inebriated conversation, she quite unequivocally exposed the hoax to the authorities.

As I boarded the plane, I felt a hundred pairs of eyes staring at me. I scanned their faces and spotted Grace flirting with her seatmate and pretending not to know me when I walked past. A few rows back, Julie and Mollie sat next to each other. They cast me looks of love and relief as I continued on by. My wife was tucked into an aisle seat, her injured arm pulled close to her chest. Angela's head rested in her lap.

Before sitting down behind them, I glanced at the back of the plane where Max stared wide-eyed out the window in eager anticipation of takeoff. He looked up at me and flashed his gigantic wild smile, revealing his triangular teeth, and then flinched and snapped his mouth shut to block out the cold air from the vent. It broke my heart.

My seat was nestled between two of the stouter humans on the planet, whose diet clearly consisted of more than just fish. I took a forlorn pause in the aisle, drawing in what might be my last dose of oxygen for several hours, and then wedged myself in. I searched in vain for the arm rests, did a bit of contorting in an attempt to soothe my aching back, and settled in.

Within minutes, the plane started taxiing slowly down the tarmac, and then it turned sharply in preparation for departure. Leaning my head back, I was suddenly overcome with a profound sense of gratitude.

We had survived our vacation from hell. Yes, one of us had nearly lost her limbs and one of us had lost his teeth, but we were all alive.

Where would we have been without all the strangers who'd come into our lives at the most perilous of times—and just as quickly disappeared without so much as a trace? And then there were the Walshes, whose unbelievable hospitality could never be repaid. Who were these selfless people? Were they even real? I might never know, but I would be eternally grateful for their generosity.

Joeline's mortality had become all too real to me. Like my own.

On the Wild West trip, none of us had a clue. We were young and indestructible—we were going to live forever. And we had only ourselves to worry about.

But throughout the years, I had regressed into a mere mortal. My body was less tolerant of strenuous activity, and I had six major responsibilities now, two of whom needed serious medical attention.

Right then, I accepted wholeheartedly—the enthusiasm would come later—that my reckless escapades were indeed over, not because they had to be, but because I wanted them to be. I was grateful for the adventures I'd had, the foolish and dangerous ones as well as the more thought out. I was even more grateful to have survived them.

The last two weeks had tested my marriage and my role as a father, caregiver, and decision maker. If this trip had taught me anything, it was just how much my wife and family meant to me, and how fragile and fleeting life was. In the end, I had achieved my goal—we'd had a memorable trip—though in a twisted way. If Joeline ever permitted us to leave the house again, we'd do it differently. Hell, maybe we really would go to the French Riviera.

What a relief to have my entire family on the plane. Although dispersed throughout the cabin, we were all going home together.

And we were next in line for takeoff.

epilogue

Kiawah Island, 2022. *Back row, left to right*: Simone (Max's girl-
friend), Max, Joeline, Angela Rizzo, Leo Rizzo, and Jeremy Rizzo;
front row, left to right: Julie, me, Mollie, Jack Ly, Mike Ly, and Grace.

In keeping with the spirit of this trip, our flight did not land at its
intended destination. Instead, we were diverted to Pittsburgh because of the weather conditions in Charlotte—or maybe because one
of the wings had fallen off. I couldn't understand the pilot's explanation in my red-eye-induced state of grogginess. This unanticipated
landing in turn necessitated the division of our family onto separate
aircraft for the final leg of the journey. Despite this annoyance, we
all arrived in Charlotte at roughly the same time. Miraculously, so
did all eighteen pieces of luggage.

Upon our return to everyday life, Joeline began losing weight rapidly. And she felt tired and weak all the time. The grueling physical
therapy for the injuries sustained to her leg and arm added to her

lethargy. The medical professionals in Charlotte couldn't diagnose the cause. One of the doctors concluded that it was PTSD and prescribed an anti-anxiety medication that Joeline refused to take. She was adamant—her condition was not psychological.

Three weeks later, Dr. Terry Nurre, Joeline's sister-in-law whom we had consulted immediately after the accident, called us to say she was convinced that Joeline had giardia—a dangerous intestinal parasite. This infection is typically contracted by drinking backcountry water, like the non-potable kind found at the Kicking Horse Campground. The diagnosis was confirmed, and Joeline began treatment immediately. Her strength and determination carried her through, and she made a full recovery.

Over the course of several years, she became a certified aquatics therapist and established a rehabilitation program for stroke victims and geriatric patients, helping them attain a level of physical activity they hadn't experienced for months or even years. She has since retired and devotes her time to her family, including her two grandsons, and her circle of friends. Although she still loves being outdoors, these days she prefers tennis and gardening to camping.

Max also contracted giardia. His symptoms weren't as severe and cleared up on their own. Our dentist repaired Max's teeth using the chips Julie had retrieved from the stream. They remained firmly embedded in his mouth for about a month—until Mollie knocked them out in a pillow fight. The pillow wasn't so much the problem as the Cabbage Patch doll he was holding in front of his face upon impact. Over the course of the next few years, his teeth were knocked out several more times. Eventually he got crowns. If you look closely, you can see a small, dark line running diagonally across both front teeth.

Max went on to graduate from the honors business program at the University of North Carolina at Charlotte and currently works as a fraud investigator. His unbridled zest for adventure has only grown over the years, and he can be found mountain biking, snowboarding, skiing, boating, running, playing volleyball, or whitewater rafting.

He still loves to camp and has done so in places like the outback of Australia as well as the peaks of Mount Hood and Mount Baker.

Julie was the child most affected by the events of the trip. To this day, it's difficult for her to talk about what happened. After graduating from the University of Chapel Hill, she packed her bags and moved to Los Angeles. For eleven years, she worked as a video editor for Entertainment Tonight and occasionally for the Dr. Phil show.

Julie moved back to Charlotte in 2013, having tired of the tinsel town scene. She now works alongside her brother in fraud investigations. She has not camped as an adult, nor is she ever likely to camp again, under any circumstances, ever.

Grace graduated from North Carolina State University and joined the Services to the Armed Forces division of the American Red Cross. She lived overseas for three years on military bases in South Korea, Iraq, and Germany. Always looking for adventure, she ran with the bulls in Spain, went dogsledding across the Arctic Circle, rode camels in both the Gobi and Sahara deserts, celebrated Carnival in Venice, floated in the Dead Sea, rode elephants in Thailand, and hiked the Diamond Mountain in North Korea.

In 2008 Grace moved to Washington, DC, to accept an appointment at the White House and was subsequently hired by the CIA as an undercover officer. She could tell you what she did, but then, well, you know the rest. She married an Asian man with a British accent whom she met on a beach in New Zealand. They live in Charlotte with their young son. Grace rides her big black Friesian horse every day and still enjoys an occasional weekend in a tent.

Mollie earned her MBA in 2011 from Wake Forest University on a full scholarship. While there, she initiated a study abroad program in Australia, spending six months "studying" the local cultures of New Zealand, Bali, and Fiji. She later earned an advanced project management certification from Stanford University—taught partly by me.

Today, Mollie resides in Seattle. As a Delta executive, she visits the Seattle airport on a regular basis, flying on a whim wherever she chooses. She has vacationed in Aruba, Bora Bora, Bermuda, India, Indonesia, China, Thailand, South Korea, Chile, Belize, and the United Arab Emirates, to name just a few. Mollie would happily go camping if someone else took care of all the logistics and did all the work, including pitching her very own private luxury tent and toasting her s'mores.

Angela followed the closest in her mother's footsteps, earning her master's degree from East Carolina University in speech pathology. She also studied in Spain for six months and traveled throughout much of Europe, as well as visiting northern Africa. She made it a priority to sample the local donuts throughout her travels and can attest that Duck Donuts, originating in the Outer Banks of North Carolina, are by far the tastiest. Now married and a stay-at-home mom to her blond-haired boy, she doesn't like to camp unless it's at the Ritz.

As for me? Well, you know, I had to use those free tickets. I wanted a redo.

In 1996, we went back to British Columbia, to the scene of the crime. We drove through Golden, directly past the hospital where Joeline was first treated, and then decided that was enough nostalgia. (For those of you keeping tabs, we paid all our medical bills—without anyone from the health insurance company ever answering the phone.)

We met up with the Walshes again and spent several glorious, disaster-free days with them at their lake house. Two years later, they visited us in North Carolina. Their children are now grown with impressive careers. The Walshes continue to live in one of the most beautiful places on earth. We have stayed in the periphery of one another's lives and remain eternally grateful for their generous hospitality.

Our final camping trip, it turns out, was in the summer of 2000. By then Julie was old enough to boycott and stay home alone, which she emphatically chose to do. And Grace elected to spend the summer working on a dude ranch in Colorado. The rest of us, along with Joeline's brother and family, set off for Alaska for two weeks, home to an estimated thirty thousand grizzly bears. Luckily, the ones we encountered weren't within clawing distance. Big Blue tagged along, though we slept most nights in Big Bessie, the RV we rented. Not a single mishap occurred on that trip—nor on any other.

Big Blue never went out west again, but our faithful companion continued to provide shelter for us at Sliding Rock in the Smokies for several more years. Eventually, the trips started taking a real toll. Despite all the Silly Putty, duct tape, and leakage sealant, the tent disintegrated beyond recognition and had to be laid to rest.

I retired from IBM in 2005 after thirty-two years. While my extreme adventures had ended years before, my geographic travels expanded. Big Blue (the corporate one) retained my services as a consultant. This gig sent me all over the world teaching leadership courses and helped me rack up forty-four country passport stamps.

I climbed the Great Wall of China and stood amid the Terra-Cotta Army, but declined an invitation to a public execution in Beijing. I rode camels and elephants en route to the Taj Mahal, walked through the ancient pyramid city of Caral, Peru, and explored the treasures of Petra and the glories of Greece and Rome. I've snorkeled along the Great Barrier Reef, as well as reefs off Belize, Lanai, Bermuda, and Cancun. I have felt the heat of volcanoes in Hawaii and Iceland and seen the Arctic Circle from both the east and the west, not to mention gazing up at the Southern Cross in New Zealand.

Would you believe IBM even sent me to the French Riviera? Joeline accompanied me on this assignment, and we tacked on several days, swimming and sightseeing along the Mediterranean.

Financing a couple of my own domestic trips, I ticked off state number fifty in Fargo, North Dakota. Apparently, I'm not the only one who visits North Dakota as their fiftieth state. The sign at the visitor center says, "You saved the best state for last." I'd been saving the Roughrider State for over forty years, ever since we drove a hundred miles south of it during our Wild West trip.

In July 2021, despite my continued fear of bears, Mollie convinced Joeline and me to join her at Brooks Falls on the Kenai peninsula of Alaska, home to thousands of grizzly bears. On one of the trails, we came face-to-face with a mamma grizzly and her cub—clearly my magnetic pull was still holding strong.

The following summer, we had a Wild West reunion to celebrate the fiftieth anniversary of our summer adventure. The other guys all still live in Cincinnati and have enjoyed meaningful careers: Couzy as a high school teacher and basketball coach, Walt in hospital administration, Woody also as a high school teacher and coach, and Mel as a successful civil engineer. Mel maintains a stricter dress code today and managed to stay fully clothed for the entire reunion.

That ten-week trip in 1972 was one of the best adventures of my life. And the two-week trip in 1994 was one of the most stressful, but it adjusted my ambitions, expectations, and priorities.

I must have done something right. Decades later, our family is a close-knit group who love and support one another. We all look back on our camping days and laugh or smile and occasionally wish we could relive one of those nights in Big Blue or slide down a cold mountain waterfall. Truly they brought us together, and we wouldn't trade them for anything.

I still love camping—the crackle of the campfire, the scent of fresh forest, the frosty mountain stream, a juicy fire-cooked sausage, the thousands of stars unfolding in the night sky. I will always love it. I am thankful for every adventure I have had, every mountain I have climbed, every stream I have crossed, every night I have spent out in the woods, and every crazy story I have lived to tell.

Most of all, though, I am thankful for my family and for every laugh we have shared, every obstacle we have overcome, and every incredible experience we have had together. They have, by far, been my greatest adventure.

acknowledgments

To my daughter Grace, this book would not exist without your ambition. Thank you for your years of hard work, dedication, and vision. Your accomplishments never cease to amaze me. I'm grateful to have worked with you on this one.

Grace and I would like to thank Sandra Jonas, our editor and publisher. It has been a pleasure to work with you. Your meticulous attention to detail, knowledge, and experience took this book to a whole new level. We are honored to have had the opportunity to collaborate with you on *Tent*!

To those who read the early manuscript and provided feedback, we greatly appreciate your time and attention. Our special thanks to Mollie Ohlhaut, Marcus Ohlhaut, and Dana Goldfarb, for your insights and comments, which proved invaluable as we finalized the book.

David Kwong, Reynold Hoover, Bill Bartee, and Ian Bondi, thank you for your early endorsements. To our marketing and publicity team, thank you for your hard work and creativity.

Our gratitude to Mike Ly, Jack Ly, Mike Moruzi, Jill Tappert, Dr. John Nurre, Dr. Terry Nurre, and Dr. James Lemmons for your assistance and encouragement.

To my Wild West buddies, our 1972 trip instilled in me a love for the outdoors that has only grown over the years. Thank you all for making it one of the best summers a guy could ever have.

To the Walsh family, your generosity made a lasting impression on us. And to everyone on that trip—angel or otherwise—who lent assistance, thank you. We might not have made it without you.

To my children, you have been my greatest joy and proudest achievement. Thank you for letting us share your characters in this book.

To my loving wife and best friend, Joeline, thank you for being my partner and for allowing me to share this part of our story.

alice and allin's saskatoon pie

In memory of Allin

Ingredients:

- 4 cups saskatoons
- 1 cup chopped rhubarb
- 2 tablespoons water
- 2 tablespoons lemon juice
- ¾ cup granulated sugar
- 1½ tablespoons quick-cooking tapioca (or 3 tablespoons corn-starch or flour)
- 2 tablespoons butter

Joeline whipping up saskatoon pie filling, 2023.

Directions:

1. Heat oven to 425°F.
2. Wash and drain saskatoons.
3. Mix saskatoons, rhubarb, water, lemon juice, sugar, and tapioca in saucepan. Simmer for a few minutes. This will thicken when cool. If the mixture is too runny, add more tapioca (or thickening agent).
4. Make pastry while ingredients simmer.
5. Pour fruit mixture into pie shell.
6. Dot fruit with thin slices of butter.
7. Cover top with pastry crust and slit or lattice.
8. Bake for 40 to 50 minutes. Remove and place on rack to cool.

Notes from Alice:

Allin always made his own crust. For a 9-inch pie: 2 cups flour, 1 teaspoon salt, ¾ cup shortening, 4 to 5 tablespoons cold water.

He was always improvising! The preliminary simmering takes the guesswork out of deciding if the berries are juicy or too dry. If they seemed juicy, he would skip adding water and lemon juice, put the mix in the pie shell, dot it with butter, add the crust, slit it and cook it.

Baked or unbaked, the pie can be frozen.

about the authors

Grace Ly and Marty Ohlhaut.

MARTY OHLHAUT worked for thirty-two years as a risk management partner with IBM and then spent the next twelve years teaching strategic execution courses around the world. He has traveled to forty-four countries as well as all fifty states, making him an encyclopedia of amazing stories and anecdotes.

His many adventures include crisscrossing Asia, touring capital cities throughout Central and South America, roaming across sixteen European countries, and living on a boat in Alaska's inside passage, fishing for weeks at a time.

Marty and his wife, Joeline, have been married for over forty years and have five grown children and two grandchildren. Originally from Cincinnati, Ohio, they now live in Charlotte, North Carolina.

GRACE LY (Marty's daughter) worked for the American Red Cross and was stationed on military bases around the world. While living abroad in South Korea, Iraq and Germany, she traveled the world extensively, visiting more than thirty countries.

Back in the States, she moved to Washington, DC, and accepted an appointment at the White House to promote and foster a culture of service and volunteerism. She continued serving her country as an undercover officer for the Central Intelligence Agency. Two years later, she rolled back her cover to pursue her passion, becoming a feature story writer in the Office of Public Affairs at the CIA.

After more than a decade away, Grace returned home to Charlotte, North Carolina, where she lives with her British husband, young son, and Friesian horse.

Made in the USA
Las Vegas, NV
17 October 2024

96997967R00146